Approach, Passage, and Survival of Juvenile Salmonids at Little Goose Dam, Washington: Post-Construction Evaluation of a Temporary Spillway Weir, 2009

By John W. Beeman, Amy C. Braatz, Hal C. Hansel, Scott D. Fielding, Philip V. Haner, Gabriel S. Hansen, Dana J. Shurtleff, Jamie M. Sprando, and Dennis W. Rondorf

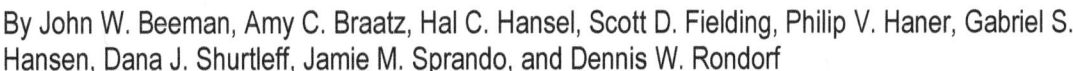

Prepared in cooperation with the U.S. Army Corps of Engineers

Open-File Report 2010-1224

U.S. Department of the Interior
U.S. Geological Survey

U.S. Department of the Interior
KEN SALAZAR, Secretary

U.S. Geological Survey
Marcia K. McNutt, Director

U.S. Geological Survey, Reston, Virginia: 2010

For more information on the USGS—the Federal source for science about the Earth, its natural and living resources, natural hazards, and the environment, visit
http://www.usgs.gov
or call 1-888-ASK-USGS.

For an overview of USGS information products, including maps, imagery, and publications, visit *http://www.usgs.gov/pubprod.*

To order this and other USGS information products, visit *http://store.usgs.gov.*

Suggested citation:
Beeman, J.W., Braatz, A.C., Hansel, H.C., Fielding, S.D., Haner, P.V., Hansen, G.S., Shurtleff, D.J., Sprando, J.M., and Rondorf, D.W., 2010, Approach, passage, and survival of juvenile salmonids at Little Goose Dam, Washington: Post-construction evaluation of a temporary spillway weir, 2009: U.S. Geological Survey Open-File Report 2010-1224, 100 p.

Contents

Figures

Tables

Conversion Factors and Datums

Conversion Factors

Inch/Pound to SI

Multiply	By	To obtain
foot (ft)	0.3048	meter (m)
cubic foot per second (ft^3/s)	0.02832	cubic meter per second (m^3/s)

SI to Inch/Pound

Multiply	By	To obtain
centimeter (cm)	0.3937	inch (in.)
millimeter (mm)	0.03937	inch (in.)
meter (m)	3.281	foot (ft)
kilometer (km)	0.6214	mile (mi)
square meter (m^2)	0.0002471	acre
liter (L)	0.2642	gallon (gal)
gram (g)	0.03527	ounce, avoirdupois (oz)

Temperature in degrees Celsius (°C) may be converted to degrees Fahrenheit (°F) as follows:

$$°F=(1.8×°C)+32.$$

Datums

Horizontal coordinate information is referenced to the World Geodetic System of 1984 (WGS84).

Vertical coordinate information is referenced to the National Geodetic Vertical Datum of 1929 (NGVD 29).

Approach, Passage, and Survival of Juvenile Salmonids at Little Goose Dam, Washington: Post-Construction Evaluation of a Temporary Spillway Weir, 2009

By John W. Beeman, Amy C. Braatz, Hal C. Hansel, Scott D. Fielding, Philip V. Haner, Gabriel S. Hansen, Dana J. Shurtleff, Jamie M. Sprando, and Dennis W. Rondorf

Executive Summary

This report describes a study of dam passage and survival of radio-tagged juvenile salmonids after installation of a temporary spillway weir (TSW) at Little Goose Dam, Washington, in 2009. The purpose of the study was to document fish passage and survival when the dam was operated with the TSW in place. Spillway weirs are one of several methods used to improve downstream passage of juvenile salmonids. Each spillway weir design is based on the concept of providing an overflow weir with a depth more similar to the natural migration depth of juvenile salmonids than conventional spill bays. Little Goose Dam was the last of the four lower Snake River dams to have a spillway weir installed. This was the first year that some form of surface passage device was operating at all Snake River and Columbia River dams between Lewiston, Idaho, and the Columbia River estuary.

The study design stipulated that a total of 30 percent of the river discharge would continuously be passed over the TSW and the conventional spill bays, and this percentage was achieved. The TSW also was to be operated at the "low crest" elevation during the spring and the "high crest" elevation during the summer, but the TSW was only operated at the low crest elevation during this study.

Behavior, passage, and survival of spring and summer juvenile salmonid migrants passing through Little Goose Dam were examined using radio telemetry. Survival was estimated using the Route Specific Survival Model (RSSM) by releasing tagged fish near Central Ferry State Park 21 kilometers upstream of the dam and in the tailrace approximately 0.5 kilometer downstream of the dam. From April 18 to May 21, 2009, 1,520 yearling Chinook salmon (*Oncorhynchus tshawytscha*) and 1,517 juvenile steelhead (*O. mykiss*) were radio tagged and released. From June 6 to July 5, 2009, 4,251 subyearling Chinook salmon (*O. tshawytscha*) were radio tagged and released. Release dates of subyearling Chinook salmon were selected to avoid "reservoir-type" fish that cease to migrate around July. Detection sites were installed in the forebay 2 kilometers upstream of the dam, on the dam, and at several sites downstream. Detection equipment was operated from April 18 to June 5, 2009, and from June 6 to July 6, 2009, hereinafter referred to as the study periods. We describe passage behaviors through the forebay, main passage routes, and tailrace, survival probabilities through the pool (release to the forebay) and forebay and passage and survival probabilities through the main passage routes (TSW, conventional spill bays, turbines, juvenile bypass), and survival passing the concrete (the dam itself) and the dam (concrete plus the forebay).

Daily discharge at Little Goose Dam during the study periods was the third highest discharge of the last 10 water years. Mean daily discharge during the spring period ranged from 61 to 165 thousand cubic feet per second (ft^3/s) with a mean of 111.6 thousand ft^3/s. Mean daily discharge during the summer study period ranged from 44 to 165 thousand ft^3/s with a mean of 93.6 thousand ft^3/s. Average daily spill was 29 percent of river discharge during the spring and 30 percent during the summer. The mean forebay elevation (633.4 feet, NGVD 29), and hence the mean discharge through the TSW (11 thousand ft^3/s), were the same during the spring and summer study periods.

As in past years, fish approach to the dam after entering the 2-kilometer forebay primarily was from the northern side of the river and forebay residence times were relatively short. Most fish were first detected upstream of the earthen dam and spillway when they were within 150–200 meters from the dam. The median forebay residence times of yearling Chinook salmon were similar to those from 2006 (about 8 hours), but forebay residence times of subyearling Chinook salmon were much shorter than in previous years. The shorter forebay residence times of subyearling Chinook salmon in 2009 compared to the other years (median 5.4 hours in 2009 versus 12.2 hours in 2006) may be due to higher discharge in 2009 than in 2006. Forebay residence times generally were shortest for fish passing through the conventional spill bays or the TSW and longest for fish passing through the powerhouse. Differences in forebay residence time may be related to the area of initial approach to the dam or the different paths fish must travel prior to entrainment in water passing the spillway versus the powerhouse. There was no evidence of a net guidance to or away from the dam along the trash/shear boom.

Dam passage rates varied by species, run timing, and passage route. Passage rates (proportion of the forebay population passing per hour) of yearling and subyearling Chinook salmon were greatest through the TSW, but the rate decreased with time spent in the forebay. Thus, there was a decrease in the passage rate through the TSW and a concomitant increase in the passage rates through the other routes the longer fish were in the forebay. Passage rates of juvenile steelhead were highest through the TSW during the day and through the bypass during the night, but yearling and subyearling Chinook salmon route-specific passage rates were similar during the day and night.

Most fish passed the dam through the TSW (tables 1, 2, and 3). The route-specific passage probabilities of yearling and subyearling Chinook salmon were similar: 62–65 percent passed through the TSW, 24 percent passed through the juvenile bypass, 7–10 percent passed through the conventional spill bays, and 4 percent passed through the turbines. Slightly more juvenile steelhead passed through the TSW (49 percent) than the juvenile bypass (41 percent), 9 percent passed through the conventional spill bays, and 1 percent passed through the turbines.

The effectiveness of the surface outlet TSW (*SOS*), or proportion of fish passage relative to water passage, was greater during the day than during the night and this difference was largest for juvenile steelhead. The estimates of *SOS* of yearling and subyearling Chinook salmon were 7.1 and 6.6 during the day and 5.2 and 3.0 during the night, respectively. Day and night estimates of *SOS* for juvenile steelhead were 7.2 and 3.0, respectively. The *SOS* of each group was 1.7–2.8 times greater than the effectiveness of the conventional spill bays (*SPS*).

The fish guidance efficiency (*FGE*), the proportion of fish entering the powerhouse that pass through the juvenile bypass, of yearling and subyearling Chinook salmon was about 0.85 whereas that of juvenile steelhead was 0.97. The *FGE*s of the juvenile salmon were higher during the day than during the night, but those of juvenile steelhead were similar during both periods. Estimates of *FGE* and other metrics in this report are based on probabilities (range 0 to 1.0) rather than percentages.

The fish passage efficiency (*FPE*), the proportion of fish passing through all non-turbine routes, was similar to other years. The *FPE* was 0.96 for yearling Chinook salmon, 0.99 for juvenile steelhead, and 0.85 for subyearling Chinook salmon.

Survival of fish was high in the pool and forebay and similar among all routes of passage other than through the turbines. Yearling Chinook salmon and juvenile steelhead pool, forebay, and route-specific survival probabilities were all greater than 0.98. Estimates of turbine survival were 0.93 for yearling Chinook salmon and 1.0 for juvenile steelhead, but these estimates were based on only 33 salmon and 11 steelhead, thus the precision of these estimates is poor. The survival of subyearling Chinook salmon generally was lower than survival of the other groups. The estimated survival probabilities for subyearling Chinook salmon were 0.92 through the pool, 0.98 through the forebay, 0.98 through the TSW, 0.85 through the conventional spill bays, 0.91 through the juvenile bypass, and 0.83 through the turbines (based on 94 fish passing through the turbines).

The operation of the low-crest TSW during 30 percent 24-hour spill at Little Goose Dam in 2009 resulted in low probabilities of turbine passage, low probabilities of passage through conventional spill bays, high probabilities of TSW passage, and high probabilities of concrete survival. The TSW was the most common route of passage, which is likely a result of the advantages inherent in surface passage devices plus its placement in an area known to have high passage rates in prior years. The addition of the TSW as a passage route at this dam provided an effective passage route with high fish survival probabilities, but did not appreciably change the *FPE* or concrete survival probability from past years. The estimates of concrete survival for yearling Chinook salmon, juvenile steelhead, and subyearling Chinook salmon met the precision goal and were greater than the minimum survivals mandated by the current Biological Opinion by the National Oceanic and Atmospheric Administration National Marine Fisheries Service.

Table 1. Passage probabilities, passage effectiveness, and survival probabilities of yearling Chinook salmon at Little Goose Dam overall and by diel period, spring 2009.

[Estimates, standard errors (SE), and 95% profile likelihood confidence intervals (95% PCI) are presented. Parameter definitions are shown in table 4. Asterisks (*) indicate the 95% PCI for the estimated difference between day and night probabilities does not include zero ($\alpha = 0.05$). Overall estimates were derived from day and night estimates weighted by the proportion of fish passing during each period. Estimates are based on detections of 535 fish passing through the TSW, 84 through spill bays 2–8, 197 through the juvenile bypass, 33 through the turbines, and 27 with an unknown passage route]

| | Parameters | Overall | | Diel period | | | | Day-Night Difference | |
| | | | | Day | | Night | | | |
		Estimate (SE)	95% PCI	Estimate(SE)	95% PCI	Estimate (SE)	95% PCI	Estimate(SE)	95% PCI
Passage Probabilities	Overall Passage	n/a	n/a	0.654 (0.016)	0.622, 0.685	0.346 (0.016)	0.316, 0.379	0.307 (0.032)	0.243, 0.370*
	Spill bays 2–8	0.099 (0.010)	0.080, 0.121	0.107 (0.013)	0.083, 0.134	0.085 (0.016)	0.057, 0.121	0.022 (0.021)	-0.021, 0.062
	TSW	0.625 (0.017)	0.592, 0.657	0.679 (0.020)	0.640, 0.718	0.522 (0.029)	0.465, 0.579	0.157 (0.035)	0.088, 0.226*
	Bays 2–8 and TSW	0.724 (0.015)	0.694, 0.754	0.786 (0.017)	0.751, 0.819	0.607 (0.029)	0.551, 0.662	0.179 (0.033)	0.114, 0.245*
	Bypass	0.237 (0.015)	0.209, 0.266	0.190 (0.017)	0.159, 0.224	0.324 (0.027)	0.273, 0.379	0.134 (0.032)	0.072, 0.198*
	Turbine	0.039 (0.007)	0.027, 0.054	0.024 (0.006)	0.013, 0.038	0.068 (0.015)	0.043, 0.101	0.045 (0.016)	0.016, 0.079*
	Powerhouse	0.276 (0.015)	0.246, 0.306	0.214 (0.017)	0.181, 0.249	0.393 (0.029)	0.338, 0.449	0.179 (0.033)	0.114, 0.245*
	FGE	0.858 (0.022)	0.809, 0.899	0.890 (0.029)	0.825, 0.938	0.826 (0.035)	0.750, 0.888	0.064 (0.046)	-0.026, 0.155
	FPE	0.961 (0.007)	0.946, 0.970	0.976 (0.006)	0.961, 0.983	0.932 (0.015)	0.899, 0.946	0.045 (0.016)	0.016, 0.079*
Effectiveness	Bays 2–8 (SPS)	0.532 (0.055)	0.431, 0.647	0.572 (0.070)	0.444, 0.719	0.458 (0.088)	0.306, 0.648	0.114 (0.112)	-0.115, 0.327
	TSW (SOS)	6.449 (0.172)	6.370, 6.600	7.077 (0.207)	6.671, 7.431	5.262 (0.294)	4.690, 5.636	1.815 (0.360)	1.271, 2.451*
	All spill (SPS)	2.554 (0.054)	2.445, 2.658	2.779 (0.062)	2.654, 2.896	2.129 (0.100)	1.969, 2.322	0.651 (0.117)	0.422, 0.882*
Survival Probabilities	Pool	0.978 (0.005)	0.967, 0.986	0.977 (0.006)	0.963, 0.987	0.980 (0.008)	0.960, 0.992	0.003 (0.010)	-0.020, 0.022
	Forebay	0.998 (0.002)	0.993, 1.000	0.998 (0.002)	0.992, 1.003	0.997 (0.004)	0.985, 1.000	0.002 (0.004)	-0.006, 0.014
	Spill bays 2–8	0.948 (0.032)	0.873, 1.000	0.941 (0.038)	0.849, 1.001	0.962 (0.058)	0.807, 1.041	0.021 (0.070)	-0.146, 0.147
	TSW	1.001 (0.011)	0.979, 1.023	0.984 (0.014)	0.955, 1.014	1.032 (0.016)	0.997, 1.067	0.048 (0.022)	0.004, 0.092*
	Bays 2–8 and TSW	0.993 (0.011)	0.973, 1.016	0.978 (0.014)	0.950, 1.008	1.022 (0.017)	0.986, 1.058	0.044 (0.022)	-0.001, 0.089
	Bypass	1.016 (0.012)	0.988, 1.040	1.018 (0.014)	0.982, 1.047	1.013 (0.023)	0.957, 1.055	0.005 (0.027)	-0.048, 0.066
	Turbine	0.928 (0.058)	0.770, 1.005	0.949 (0.077)	0.722, 1.031	0.889 (0.084)	0.685, 1.009	0.060 (0.114)	-0.202, 0.292
	Powerhouse	1.004 (0.014)	0.973, 1.030	1.011 (0.016)	0.972, 1.041	0.991 (0.025)	0.934, 1.037	0.020 (0.030)	-0.039, 0.083
	Dam	0.992 (0.010)	0.971, 1.013	0.983 (0.013)	0.958, 1.012	1.007 (0.017)	0.972, 1.043	0.024 (0.022)	-0.020, 0.067
	Concrete	0.994 (0.010)	0.974, 1.015	0.985 (0.013)	0.960, 1.013	1.010 (0.017)	0.976, 1.046	0.025 (0.021)	-0.018, 0.068

Table 2. Passage probabilities, passage effectiveness, and survival probabilities of juvenile steelhead at Little Goose Dam overall and by diel period, spring 2009.

[Estimates, standard errors (SE), and 95% profile likelihood confidence intervals (95% PCI) are presented. Parameter definitions are shown in table 4. Asterisks (*) indicate the 95% PCI for the estimated difference between day and night probabilities does not include zero (α = 0.05). Overall estimates were derived from day and night estimates weighted by the proportion of fish passing during each period. Estimates are based on detections of 413 fish passing through the TSW, 79 through spill bays 2–8, 197 through the juvenile bypass, 9 through the turbines, and 25 with an unknown passage route]

	Parameters	Overall		Day		Night		Day-Night Difference	
		Estimate(SE)	95% PCI	Estimate(SE)	95% PCI	Estimate(SE)	95% PCI	Estimate(SE)	95% PCI
Passage Probabilities	Overall Passage	n/a	n/a	0.564 (0.017)	0.531, 0.596	0.436 (0.017)	0.404, 0.469	0.127 (0.034)	0.061 0.193*
	Spill bays 2–8	0.092 (0.010)	0.074, 0.113	0.038 (0.009)	0.023, 0.057	0.163 (0.019)	0.128, 0.203	0.126 (0.021)	0.086, 0.168*
	TSW	0.489 (0.017)	0.455, 0.522	0.691 (0.021)	0.649, 0.732	0.227 (0.022)	0.187, 0.272	0.464 (0.030)	0.403, 0.522*
	Bays 2–8 and TSW	0.581 (0.017)	0.548, 0.614	0.728 (0.020)	0.687, 0.767	0.390 (0.025)	0.342, 0.440	0.338 (0.032)	0.274, 0.401*
	Bypass	0.406 (0.017)	0.374, 0.439	0.267 (0.020)	0.229, 0.308	0.586 (0.025)	0.535, 0.635	0.318 (0.033)	0.253, 0.381*
	Turbine	0.013 (0.004)	0.007, 0.022	0.004 (0.003)	-0.017, 0.013	0.024 (0.008)	0.015, 0.043	0.020 (0.008)	0.005, 0.039*
	Powerhouse	0.419 (0.017)	0.386, 0.452	0.272 (0.020)	0.233, 0.313	0.610 (0.025)	0.560, 0.658	0.338 (0.032)	0.274, 0.401*
	FGE	0.969 (0.009)	0.948, 0.976	0.985 (0.011)	0.954, 0.998	0.961 (0.013)	0.930, 0.981	0.024 (0.017)	-0.013, 0.059
	FPE	0.987 (0.004)	0.978, 0.989	0.996 (0.003)	0.987, 0.999	0.976 (0.008)	0.957, 0.983	0.020 (0.008)	0.005, 0.039*
Effectiveness	Bays 2–8 (SPS)	0.495 (0.053)	0.398, 0.606	0.200 (0.046)	0.122, 0.304	0.877 (0.103)	0.688, 1.090	0.677 (0.113)	0.464, 0.906*
	TSW (SOS)	5.060 (0.177)	4.720, 5.365	7.199 (0.221)	6.796, 7.611	2.296 (0.219)	1.897, 2.518	4.903 (0.311)	4.692, 5.299*
	All spill (SPS)	2.049 (0.060)	1.932, 2.165	2.574 (0.072)	2.428, 2.711	1.370 (0.089)	1.199, 1.546	1.204 (0.114)	0.977, 1.425*
Survival Probabilities	Pool	0.986 (0.004)	0.977, 0.993	0.986 (0.005)	0.973, 0.994	0.987 (0.006)	0.972, 0.995	0.001 (0.008)	-0.016, 0.017
	Forebay	0.990 (0.002)	0.990, 0.999	0.996 (0.003)	0.987, 0.999	0.997 (0.003)	0.988, 1.000	0.001 (0.004)	-0.009, 0.011
	Spill bays 2–8	0.997 (0.008)	0.973, 1.008	1.000 (0.000)	1.000, 1.000	0.994 (0.017)	0.939, 1.019	0.006 (0.017)	-0.019, 0.061
	TSW	0.998 (0.006)	0.980, 1.008	0.997 (0.003)	0.987, 1.000	0.999 (0.013)	0.958, 1.021	0.001 (0.014)	-0.039, 0.025
	Bays 2–8 and TSW	0.997 (0.005)	0.984, 1.007	0.997 (0.003)	0.987, 1.000	0.997 (0.011)	0.967, 1.018	0.001 (0.012)	-0.021, 0.030
	Bypass	0.994 (0.007)	0.975, 1.005	0.984 (0.011)	0.952, 0.998	1.006 (0.008)	0.988, 1.024	0.021 (0.013)	-0.002, 0.056
	Turbine	1.005 (0.003)	1.001, 1.012	1.000 (0.000)	1.000, 1.000	1.010 (0.006)	1.002, 1.028	0.010 (0.006)	0.002, 0.027*
	Powerhouse	0.994 (0.007)	0.975, 1.005	0.984 (0.011)	0.953, 0.998	1.006 (0.008)	0.989, 1.024	0.021 (0.013)	-0.002, 0.056
	Dam	0.994 (0.004)	0.984, 1.003	0.990 (0.005)	0.978, 0.996	0.999 (0.008)	0.983, 1.018	0.010 (0.009)	-0.009, 0.031
	Concrete	0.998 (0.004)	0.989, 1.006	0.994 (0.004)	0.984, 0.999	1.002 (0.008)	0.987, 1.021	0.008 (0.008)	-0.008, 0.028

Table 3. Passage probabilities, passage effectiveness, and survival probabilities of subyearling Chinook salmon at Little Goose Dam overall and by diel period, summer 2009.

[Estimates, standard errors (SE), and 95% profile likelihood confidence intervals (95% PCI) are presented. Parameter definitions are shown in table 4. Asterisks (*) indicate the 95% PCI for the estimated difference between day and night probabilities does not include zero ($\alpha = 0.05$). Overall estimates were derived from day and night estimates weighted by the proportion of fish passing during each period. Estimates are based on detections of 1,398 fish passing through the TSW, 149 through spill bays 2–8, 528 through the juvenile bypass, 94 through the turbines, and 273 with an unknown passage route]

	Parameters	Overall		Diel period Day		Night		Day-Night Difference	
		Estimate(SE)	95% PCI	Estimate(SE)	95% PCI	Estimate(SE)	95% PCI	Estimate(SE)	95% PCI
Passage Probabilities	Overall Passage	n/a	n/a	0.682 (0.009)	0.663, 0.700	0.318 (0.009)	0.300, 0.337	0.364 (0.013)	0.327, 0.400*
	Spill bays 2–8	0.068 (0.005)	0.058, 0.079	0.054 (0.006)	0.043, 0.066	0.097 (0.011)	0.077, 0.120	0.043 (0.005)	0.019, 0.068*
	TSW	0.646 (0.010)	0.627, 0.666	0.780 (0.011)	0.758, 0.800	0.361 (0.018)	0.326, 0.397	0.419 (0.021)	0.377, 0.460*
	Bays 2-8 and TSW	0.714 (0.010)	0.695, 0.733	0.834 (0.010)	0.814, 0.852	0.458 (0.019)	0.421, 0.495	0.376 (0.021)	0.334, 0.418*
	Bypass	0.244 (0.009)	0.226, 0.262	0.157 (0.009)	0.139, 0.176	0.430 (0.019)	0.393, 0.467	0.273 (0.021)	0.232, 0.315*
	Turbine	0.042 (0.004)	0.034, 0.051	0.009 (0.003)	0.007, 0.015	0.112 (0.012)	0.090, 0.137	0.103 (0.012)	0.080, 0.128*
	Powerhouse	0.286 (0.010)	0.267, 0.305	0.166 (0.010)	0.148, 0.186	0.542 (0.019)	0.505, 0.579	0.376 (0.021)	0.334, 0.418*
	FGE	0.852 (0.014)	0.824, 0.879	0.943 (0.015)	0.909, 0.967	0.793 (0.021)	0.750, 0.831	0.150 (0.025)	0.100, 0.199*
	FPE	0.958 (0.004)	0.949, 0.960	0.991 (0.003)	0.985, 1.037	0.888 (0.012)	0.863, 0.909	0.103 (0.012)	0.080, 0.128*
Effectiveness	Bays 2–8 (SPS)	0.383 (0.030)	0.326, 0.445	0.307 (0.033)	0.246, 0.377	0.544 (0.062)	0.431, 0.674	0.237 (0.071)	0.103, 0.381*
	TSW (SOS)	5.431 (0.085)	5.263, 5.588	6.551 (0.090)	6.370, 6.724	3.032 (0.154)	2.735, 3.335	3.519 (0.179)	3.379, 3.863*
	All spill (SPS)	2.417 (0.032)	2.352, 2.480	2.826 (0.033)	2.760, 2.888	1.541 (0.064)	1.416, 1.667	1.285 (0.072)	1.144, 1.423*
Survival Probabilities	Pool	0.922 (0.006)	0.911, 0.933	0.922 (0.007)	0.908, 0.934	0.924 (0.010)	0.903, 0.941	0.002 (0.012)	-0.022, 0.025
	Forebay	0.984 (0.003)	0.977, 0.990	0.980 (0.004)	0.971, 0.988	0.992 (0.005)	0.980, 1.001	0.012 (0.007)	-0.002, 0.025
	Spill bays 2–8	0.852 (0.044)	0.762, 0.932	0.839 (0.057)	0.720, 0.942	0.880 (0.062)	0.750, 0.991	0.041 (0.084)	-0.125, 0.205
	TSW	0.975 (0.015)	0.945, 1.006	0.974 (0.017)	0.941, 1.010	0.977 (0.031)	0.914, 1.036	0.003 (0.035)	-0.069, 0.070
	Bays 2–8 and TSW	0.963 (0.015)	0.934, 0.991	0.966 (0.017)	0.933, 1.000	0.957 (0.029)	0.899, 1.012	0.009 (0.033)	-0.056, 0.076
	Bypass	0.908 (0.024)	0.859, 0.955	0.877 (0.033)	0.810, 0.940	0.976 (0.029)	0.918, 1.031	0.099 (0.044)	0.013, 0.186*
	Turbine	0.828 (0.096)	0.623, 0.980	0.812 (0.138)	0.518, 1.027	0.861 (0.059)	0.739, 0.968	0.049 (0.150)	-0.204, 0.364
	Powerhouse	0.898 (0.024)	0.851, 0.944	0.873 (0.032)	0.808, 0.935	0.952 (0.027)	0.898, 1.005	0.079 (0.042)	-0.003, 0.163
	Dam	0.936 (0.013)	0.911, 0.963	0.932 (0.017)	0.900, 0.965	0.947 (0.022)	0.904, 0.990	0.015 (0.027)	-0.039, 0.069
	Concrete	0.952 (0.013)	0.926, 0.978	0.950 (0.017)	0.919, 0.984	0.954 (0.022)	0.911, 0.998	0.004 (0.013)	-0.050, 0.058

Introduction

As the operator of hydroelectric dams on the Lower Snake and Columbia Rivers, the U.S. Army Corps of Engineers (USACE) has been required to evaluate the recovery of anadromous fish within the framework of the Endangered Species Act and comply with the Biological Opinions of the National Oceanic and Atmospheric Administration's National Marine Fisheries Service (NOAA Fisheries). The Biological Opinions define specific actions to evaluate to improve survival of salmon and steelhead in the Snake and Columbia Rivers. One of these actions included investigation of surface bypass technologies to safely pass juvenile salmonids over dams.

Over the past decade, the USACE has tested, refined, and implemented surface bypass technologies as a viable alternative passage route to conventional spillways, turbines, and bypass systems for the safe downstream passage of juvenile salmonids. Surface bypass technologies capitalize on the natural tendency of juvenile salmonids to migrate at shallow depths (Cash and others, 2005; Beeman and Maule, 2006). Observations at several Columbia River Basin dams have shown that out-migrating juvenile salmonids pass through surface-oriented structures at higher rates per unit of water volume discharged than the relatively deeper turbine or spillway passage routes (Johnson and others, 1992; Swan and others, 1995; Adams and Counihan, 2009). The year 2009 marked the first time there were surface passage routes at each of the eight dams from Lower Granite Dam on the Snake River, near Lewiston, Idaho, to Bonneville Dam on the Columbia River, near Cascade Locks, Oregon. These passage devices, apart from the ice-trash sluiceway at The Dalles Dam, were designed based on the concept of a shallow entrance with gradually increasing velocities upstream of a weir crest described by Haro and others (1998).

Little Goose Dam was the last of the eight Federal Snake River and Columbia River dams between Lewiston, Idaho, and the Columbia River estuary to be fitted with a surface passage route. The weir at Little Goose Dam was installed during the spring of 2009. It was designed as a temporary spillway weir (TSW), which is a simpler and less expensive design than the removable spillway weirs that have been installed at some other dams. The TSW at Little Goose Dam is a shaped crest that is lowered atop of a series of bulkheads in an otherwise conventional spill bay. In 2009, there also were TSWs at McNary and John Day Dams, although each was based on a unique design. The TSW at Little Goose Dam is unique because it was designed to be operated at either of two elevations. This capability was designed so that during periods of low river discharge, generally during the summer, the amount of water passed over the TSW could be reduced, leaving more water available for passing through conventional spill bays for control of tailrace conditions. The TSW was placed in spill bay 1, which is the bay nearest the powerhouse. Placing the TSW in bay 1 was consistent with studies in 2006 and 2007 that indicated a high probability of passage in that area (Beeman and others, 2008a, 2008b).

During 2009, radio telemetry was used to examine behavior, passage, and survival of spring and summer juvenile salmonids migrating past Little Goose Dam. This study followed a study of direct injury and survival of fish using balloon tags prior to the fish migration season (Normandeau and others, 2009). Our objectives were (1) to determine the approach path, route of passage, and tailrace egress of spring and summer migrants during operation of the TSW and 24-h 30% spill and (2) to estimate the route-specific survival of spring and summer migrants through Little Goose Dam.

Description of Study Area

Little Goose Dam is located 113 river kilometers (rkm, 70 mi) upstream of the confluence of the Snake and Columbia Rivers (fig. 1). The reservoir formed by Little Goose Dam (Lake Bryant) extends 60 rkm (37 mi) upstream to Lower Granite Dam. The river downstream of Little Goose Dam (Lake Herbert G. West) is impounded by Lower Monumental Dam located 46 rkm (29 mi) downstream of Little Goose Dam. Our study area extended from the release point at Central Ferry Bridge located 21 rkm (13 mi) upstream of Little Goose Dam, downstream to a detection site at Lower Monumental Dam (fig. 2).

Little Goose Dam is composed of four primary structures: a powerhouse, spillway, navigation lock, and earthen dam (fig. 3). The spillway consists of eight spill bays, each with a Tainter gate to regulate discharge. Water is discharged at the ogee crest, about 16 m (52 ft) deep. A TSW was installed during spring 2009 in spill bay 1, adjacent to the powerhouse (fig. 4). The powerhouse consists of six turbine units and is capable of generating 810 megawatts. The top of each turbine intake is about 19 m (61 ft) deep and divided into three slots. Each slot is partially occluded by an extended-length submersible bar screen (ESBS) that guides some downstream migrating salmonids away from the turbines into a juvenile fish collection channel and juvenile fish facility. A trash/shear boom, about 2 m deep, floats at an angle in front of the powerhouse to guide surface debris toward the spillway (fig. 3).

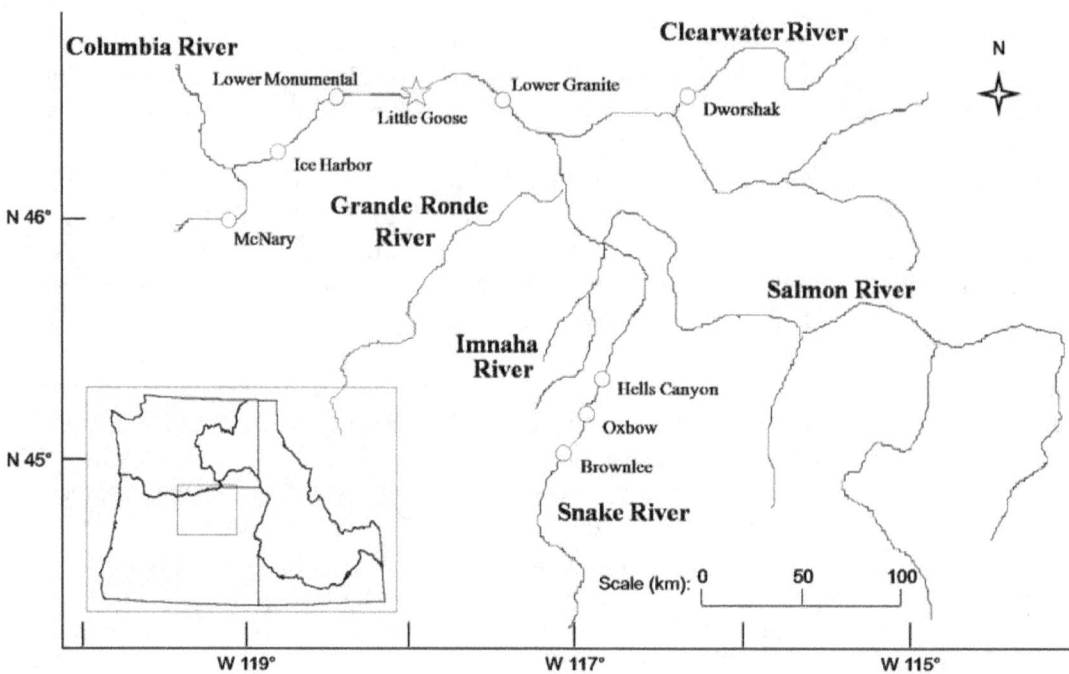

Figure 1. Map showing overview of the Snake River and its major tributaries and the location of Little Goose Dam relative to other major hydroelectric projects in the region.

8

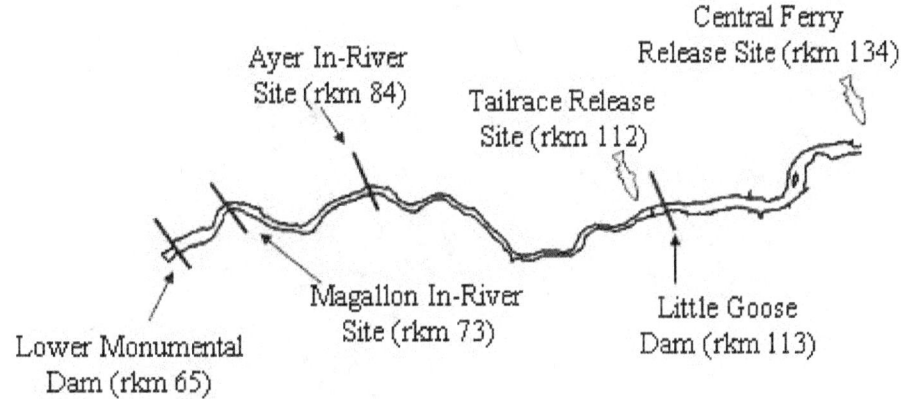

Figure 2. Diagram showing Little Goose Dam, fish release sites (fish symbol) and in-river survival arrays (lines) during the spring and summer study periods in 2009. River flow is from right to left. Rkm is the river kilometer measured from the confluence of the Snake and Columbia Rivers.

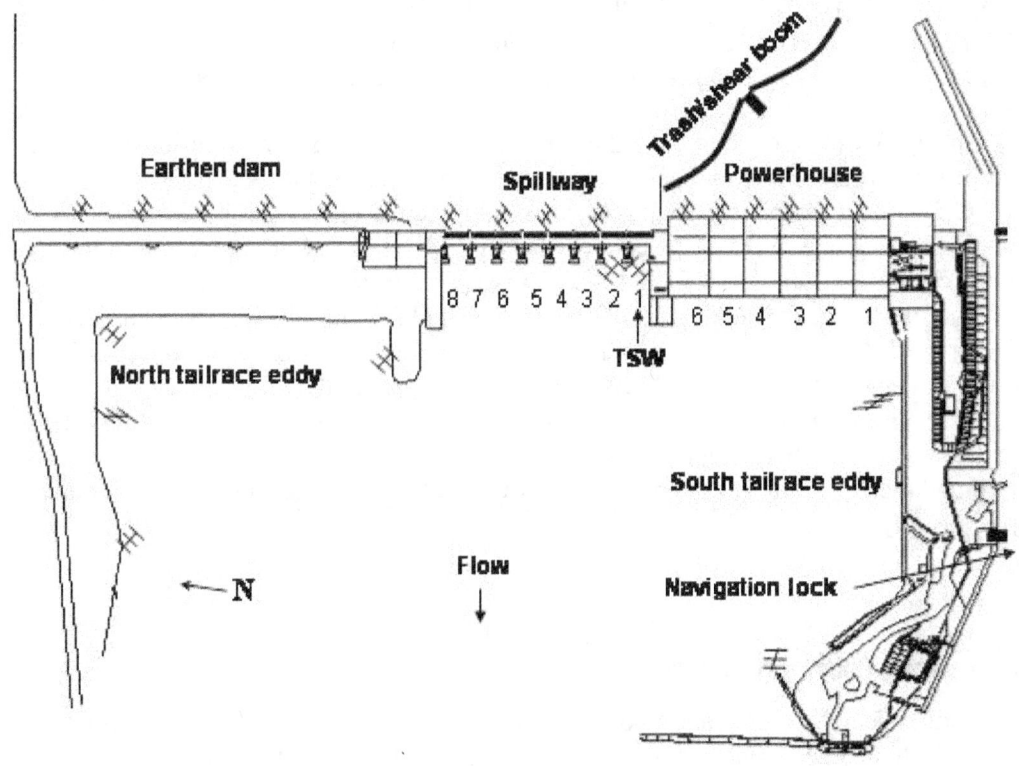

Figure 3. Schematic of aerial antennas located on the earthen dam, spillway, temporary spillway weir (TSW), powerhouse, and north and south tailrace eddies, Little Goose Dam, 2009.

Figure 4. Photograph of spill bays 1 through 4 looking upstream, Little Goose Dam, 2009. The temporary spillway weir (TSW) is installed in spill bay 1, adjacent to the powerhouse. (Photograph taken by Amy Braatz, U.S. Geological Survey, Cook, Washington, June 8, 2009.)

The TSW can be operated at either of two elevations. The two elevations allow the amount of water passed over the weir to be adjusted relative to total river flow. The operation at Little Goose Dam during the fish passage season typically consists of a total of 30% of total river discharge passed over the conventional spill bays and weir. Operation of the weir at the low crest elevation of 618 ft (188.3 m; NGVD 29) results in about 11 thousand ft³/s passing over the weir at a forebay elevation of 633.5 ft (193.1 m; NGVD 29). Operation at the high crest elevation of 622 ft (189.6 m; NGVD 29) results in 8 thousand ft³/s passing over the weir, allowing more water to be passed through conventional spill bays to aid in control of the tailrace hydraulic conditions. The *a-priori* plan of operation in 2009 was to use the low crest elevation during the spring until 3 consecutive days of flow less than 75 thousand ft³/s occurred and then to change to the high crest elevation. In 2009, the change in weir elevation occurred on July 7.

Methods

Radio Telemetry Receiving Systems

Radio telemetry antennas and data-logging receivers were installed throughout the study area with the intent of monitoring fish behavior, route-specific passage, and route-specific survival through the dam. The type of equipment used at a particular site was largely dependent on which of these three objectives was appropriate for that location. Antennas were either aerial Yagi-Uda; or underwater stripped coax, dipole or armored dipole (Beeman and others, 2004), and signal acquisition at each antenna was logged using either Lotek SRX_400-W16 receivers (Lotek Wireless, Inc.©, New Market, Ontario, Canada), Orion receivers (Sigma Eight Inc.©, Richmond Hill, Ontario, Canada), or Multi-protocol Integrated Telemetry Acquisition Systems (MITAS, Sigma Eight Inc.©, Richmond Hill, Ontario, Canada).

Arrays to monitor fish behavior were deployed at the forebay entrance (rkm 115), Little Goose Dam (earthen dam, spillway, TSW, trash/shear boom, powerhouse, adult ladder, north tailrace, and the south tailrace wall; figs. 3 and 5), and the tailrace exit (rkm 111). The aerial array used at the earthen dam in past studies was at a higher elevation than those at the spillway and powerhouse, which resulted in unequal detection ranges among areas. To reduce this difference, we installed a new earthen dam array at the same forebay elevation and antenna angle as the aerial arrays on the spillway and powerhouse. This new array, combined with the aerial spillway and powerhouse arrays, detected spring fish within 200 m and summer fish within 150 m from the dam. The old earthen dam array was left in place to facilitate comparisons between the new array used in 2009 and the old array used in past studies. We monitored fish near each of the 20 floating sections of the trash/shear boom with MITAS and single underwater dipole antennas on each section and monitored fish near the attachment frame with eight stripped coax antennas (fig. 5). The adult ladder site consisted of four stripped coax antennas in pool number 563 of the south adult ladder monitored by two Orion receivers (fig. 5). All aerial antennas were monitored using SRX receivers with the exception of the tailrace TSW aerial antennas, which were monitored by Orion receivers (fig. 3).

Route-specific passage arrays were deployed in all spill bays including the TSW, all turbine intake slots on the ESBS, and within the juvenile fish collection channel (figs. 5, 6, and 7). Each spill bay was monitored with eight underwater dipole antennas. The TSW also was monitored with 16 stripped coax antennas on the surface (fig. 7). The ESBS had four armored underwater dipole antennas, and the juvenile fish collection channel was monitored using four armored underwater dipole antennas (two on each of the downstream orifices of turbine units 1 and 2). Antennas were divided into two independent, redundant arrays for each passage route for the Route Specific Survival Model (RSSM; Skalski and others, 2002). Passage arrays used underwater dipole antennas, which have a shorter detection range (6–10 m) than aerial antennas (100–300 m, depending on tag depth; Johnson and others, 2000), in order to more precisely estimate fish passage location and increase the confidence that fish detected in a route were committed to passage there. Tailrace eddies (Jepson and others, 2009) were monitored with aerial antennas. Aerial antennas along the north eddy were placed to monitor north of spill bay 8 and downstream of the earthen dam approximately 400 m. Aerial antennas along the south eddy were located on the upstream outfall of the juvenile fish facility south of spill bay 1 approximately 100 m downstream of the dam.

We used three detection sites downstream of the dam to detect fish for estimating survival. These sites were located (1) near Ayer, Washington (rkm 84), (2) near Magallon Road, Washington (rkm 73), and (3) in the tailrace of Lower Monumental Lock and Dam (rkm 65, fig. 2). Site selection criteria are presented in section, "Estimating Passage and Survival Parameters." Signal acquisition at survival arrays was through aerial antennas and data were logged using multiple SRX receivers to reduce scan time.

Sites were visited every 1 to 2 days throughout the study period for data collection, maintenance, and troubleshooting. Data were downloaded from SRX receivers using handheld and laptop computers in conjunction with wireless 900 MHz modems (Digi International, Inc.©, Minnetonka, Minnesota). Data recorded by the MITAS were written directly to a computer hard drive. All data were backed up prior to transfer from the field to our office.

A passive integrated transponder (PIT tag) was inserted into the body cavity of each fish during surgical implantation of the radio tag so we could use the PIT tag detection system at Little Goose Dam to increase detection probabilities through the Little Goose Dam juvenile bypass system, hereinafter referred to as bypass, as well as divert tagged fish back to the river for estimating survival through the bypass. Specific locations of PIT tag readers at Little Goose Dam can be found at the Pacific States Marine Fisheries Commission website (*http://www.ptagis.org/ptagis/index.jsp*).

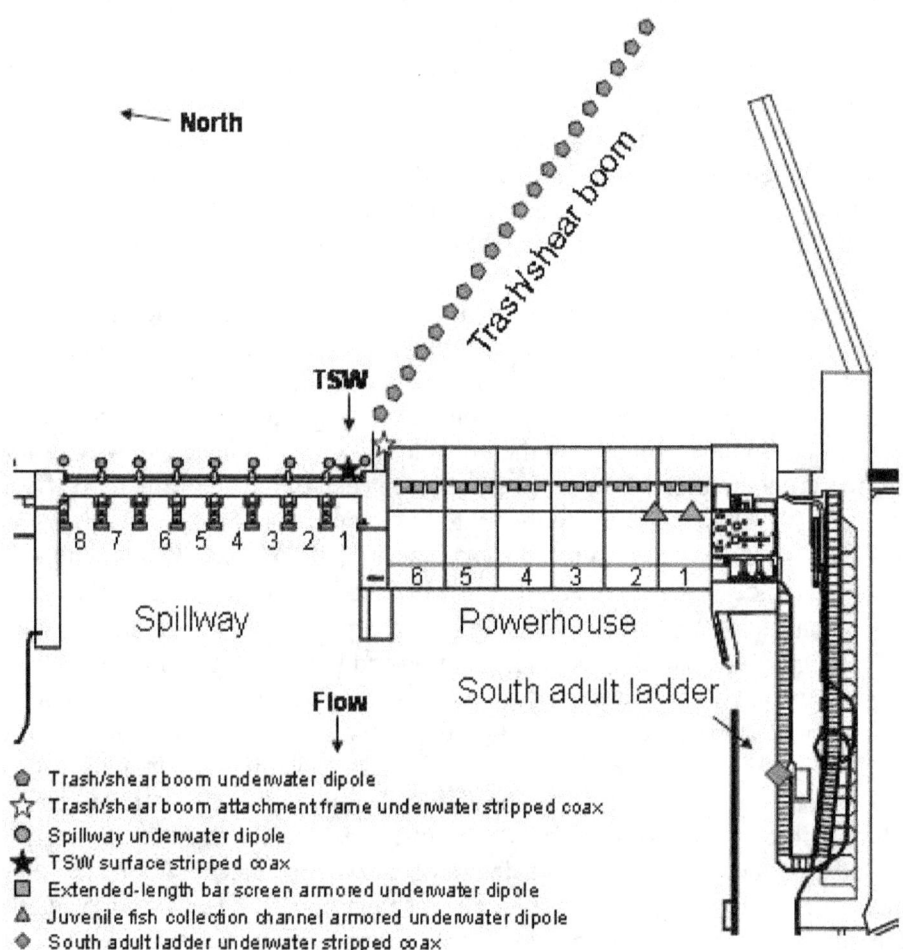

Figure 5. Schematic of underwater antennas on the spillway, temporary spillway weir (TSW), trash/shear boom, powerhouse (extended-length submersible bar screens and juvenile fish collection channel), and adult ladder, Little Goose Dam, 2009.

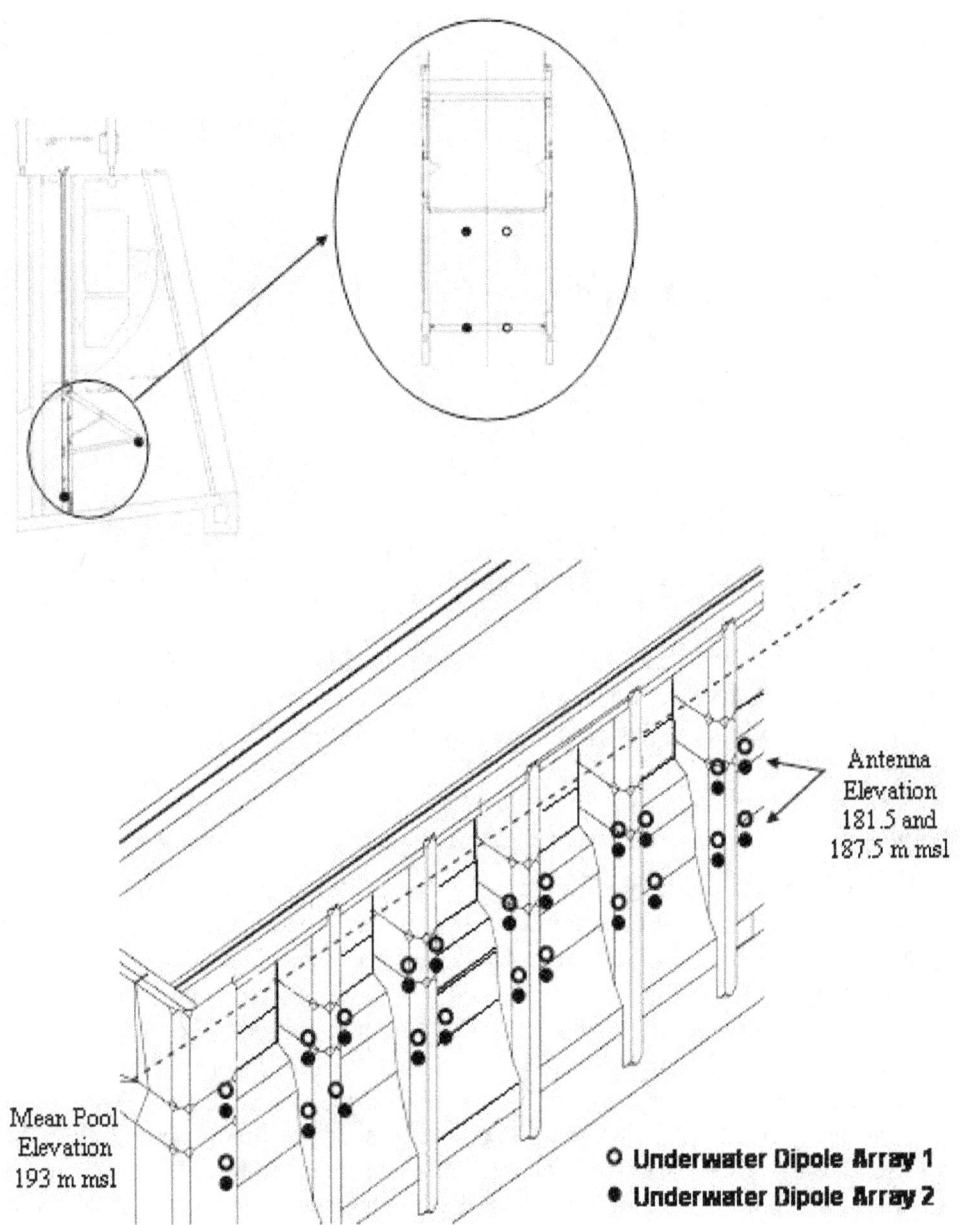

Figure 6. Schematic showing side and front views of the extended-length submersible bar screen showing underwater dipole antenna locations (upper plate) and location of underwater antennas on the spillway (lower plate), Little Goose Dam, 2009. Upper plate provided by U.S. Army Corps of Engineers.

Figure 7. Photograph of the forebay antenna deployment at the Temporary Spillway Weir in spill bay one, Little Goose Dam, 2009. Photograph is taken from the powerhouse looking north towards the spillway and earthen dam. (Photograph taken by John Beeman, U.S. Geological Survey, Cook, Washington, June 3, 2009.)

Transmitters

We used 1.5-volt digitally encoded radio transmitters and PIT tags. The radio transmitters, manufactured by Lotek Wireless, Inc.[©], were operated at frequencies between 150.340 and 150.750 MHz and used the Lotek "2003 code set." The radio transmitters used in the spring study (model NTC-3-1, weight 0.64 g in air, 16 cm "S1" antenna, 6.3 × 14.5 mm) emitted a radio signal every 2 s whereas the radio transmitters used in the summer (model NTC-M-2, 0.43 g in air, 16 cm "S1" antenna, 5.3 × 13.5 mm) emitted a radio signal every 2.5 s. The expected battery life of both transmitter types was 20 days. The PIT tags (Destron Fearing[©], model TX1411ST; St. Paul, Minnesota), emitted a unique digitally encoded signal at 134.2 kHz when activated by an electromagnetic field at a PIT-tag detector. PIT tags were 2.07 mm in diameter × 12.5 mm long and weighed 0.10 g in air. The combined tag weight was used to establish a minimum fish weight. The minimum weight was based on a maximum tag-to-fish weight ratio of approximately 5% in air; these minimums were 14.2 g for yearling Chinook salmon (*Oncorhynchus tshawytscha*) and juvenile steelhead (*O. mykiss*), and 10.0 g for subyearling Chinook salmon *(O. tshawytscha)*.

14

Tagging

Yearling hatchery spring Chinook salmon, hatchery juvenile steelhead, and hatchery and wild subyearling Chinook salmon were obtained from the juvenile fish facility sampled by the Oregon Department of Fish and Wildlife (ODFW) at Little Goose Dam. Hatchery yearling Chinook salmon and juvenile steelhead were identified by adipose fin clips or eroded fins, but there is no method to separate wild and hatchery subyearling Chinook salmon. These fish will hereinafter be referred to as yearling Chinook salmon, juvenile steelhead, and subyearling Chinook salmon. Fish were held inside the juvenile fish facility, with Chinook salmon in 265 L rectangular metal tanks and steelhead in 340 L circular fiberglass tanks at densities of less than 20 g fish/ L of water. Holding tanks were supplied with flow-through river water at all times and fish were held for approximately 24 h prior to tagging. Fish were considered suitable for tagging if they met the minimum weight criteria, were free of major injuries, had no external signs of gas bubble trauma, such as bubbles visible in fins, were no more than 20% descaled, were free of abnormalities, and had no other tags.

To implant the transmitter, fish were anesthetized using buffered ($NaHCO_3$) tricane methanesulfonate (MS-222, Argent Chemical Laboratories, Redmond, Washington) at a dosage of 65–70 mg/L. Fish were weighed to the nearest 0.1 g and fork length was measured to the nearest millimeter. Transmitters were surgically implanted using methods described by Adams and others (1998) with the exception that oxytetracycline and antibacterial ointments are no longer used. A PIT tag was placed inside the body cavity with the radio transmitter. All weighing, measuring, and containment equipment was treated with a 25 % concentration of Stress Coat® (Aquarium Pharmaceuticals, Inc©, Chalfont, Pennsylvania) to reduce handling-related stress to the fish through electrolyte loss.

Immediately following the tagging procedure, fish were placed in a 19 L perforated recovery bucket filled with 7 L of river water with dissolved oxygen levels between 120 and 150%. Each recovery bucket held a maximum of three Chinook salmon or a maximum of two steelhead. Fish were kept in the hyper-oxygenated water for a minimum of 10 min allowing them to fully recover from anesthesia. Buckets were then fitted with lids and placed in a covered raceway shaded from direct sunlight, and provided with a constant flow of river water. Fish were held between 22 and 32 h prior to release. Perforated recovery buckets ensured water circulation and were fitted with a rubber inner tube around the top of the bucket to prevent submerging completely, allowing fish access to the surface.

Fish Releases

Replicate releases of treatment and control groups of radio-tagged fish were done to estimate survival and monitor fish behavior. Treatment groups were released mid-river between U.S. Coast Guard navigation markers #12 and #13 approximately 21 km upstream of Little Goose Dam near Central Ferry State Park (rkm 134; 46° 37' 25.43"N, 117° 48' 53.63"W). Control groups were released in the Little Goose Dam tailrace about 500 m downstream of the junction of the powerhouse and spillway (rkm 112; 46° 35' 03.60" N, 118° 01' 59.64" W). Although daily release numbers varied, a ratio of 1.5:1 (on average) between treatment and control releases was maintained (see appendix A for the size of each release). An average of 27 yearling Chinook salmon (standard deviation, SD = 1.4) per treatment and 18 yearling Chinook salmon (SD = 1.0) per control group were released on each of 34 consecutive days for a total sample size of 1,470 radio-tagged yearling Chinook salmon. An average of 27 juvenile steelhead (SD = 2.2) per treatment and 18 juvenile steelhead (SD = 1.4) per control group were released on each of 34 consecutive days for a total sample size of 1,467 radio-tagged juvenile steelhead. An average of 92 subyearling Chinook salmon (SD = 30.5) per treatment and 56 subyearling Chinook salmon (SD = 17.0) per control group were released on each of 30 consecutive days for a total sample size of 4,201 radio-tagged subyearling Chinook salmon. Fluctuations in number of released fish was due to changes in fish size and number of fish passing the dam that created difficulty in consistent collection of the required number of fish each day. Release times were at four discrete time periods to ensure fish arrived at the dam over all hours of the day and night. Because the releases could not be conducted simultaneously, we alternated between releasing treatment fish and control fish first. Sample sizes were determined months before the study began by estimating the expected precision of survival estimates with the goal of species-specific estimates of juvenile salmonids surviving the dam with a standard error of less than or equal to 0.015 per the contractual agreement.

Euthanized fish were released simultaneously with the control group to estimate the probability of false-positive detections at telemetry arrays downstream of Little Goose Dam. Fifty euthanized, radio-tagged fish of each of the three species studied were released randomly throughout their respective study periods during day and night; five of each species were added to 10 releases downstream of Little Goose Dam (appendix A). We clipped gill arches and pithed each euthanized fish after 30 min in 7 L of river water containing 200 mg/L of buffered MS-222. Euthanized fish were handled and released exactly the same as live control group fish.

Release methods and transport times of treatment and control fish were similar. Recovery buckets were removed from the raceway, inspected for mortalities and malfunctioning tags and were then transferred into an insulated 1,556 L plastic tank for transportation to the release sites. The tank was filled with river water supplied with bottled oxygen to maintain 80–130% saturation in the tank and the fish were transported by truck. The release sites of treatment and control groups were different distances from the dam, so the transport time of the control group was extended to equal that of the treatment group (about 60 min). The buckets containing fish were then transferred onto a boat and motored to the release site in the middle of the river channel. At the release location, crew members removed the lids and submerged the buckets in the river, gently tipping the bucket to allow fish to swim out.

Analyses

Proofing

Prior to analysis, release and detection data were checked for quality assurance and quality control. Data were imported into SAS® (version 9.1, SAS Institute Inc.©, Cary, North Carolina) for more detailed proofing and analysis. Release and detection data were merged to create a single dataset that could be scrutinized by an automated proofing program. This automated program first removed records with invalid transmitter codes (environmental noise), duplicate records, and records collected prior to the known release date and time. The program then sequentially flagged records that met the following criteria: less than minimum signal strength, data collection after the maximum tag life (see appendix B), and less than one other corroborating detection within a ± 5-min period for a given geographic area. Because each radio-tagged fish also had a PIT tag, upstream detections occurring after known detections in a downstream juvenile fish facility also were flagged as invalid records.

After determining the validity of each record based on the criteria previously described, a fish's entire remaining detection history was flagged for manual proofing if it was suspect because of abnormally short travel times between two detection arrays or an apparent illogical sequence of detection events among geographic areas over time. Travel times were calculated as the elapsed time between the first detection at one array and the first detection at each subsequent downstream array. For travel time criteria, the probability of each fish's travel time was estimated at, or between, each location. To estimate this probability, we fit the cumulative inverse Gaussian distribution to the observed travel time distributions (Zabel, 1994; Zabel and Anderson, 1997). If the probability of a fish's travel time was less than or equal to 0.05 then these records were flagged for manual proofing. The geographic criterion was used to flag records for manual proofing based on inconsistencies in the timing and geographic location of detections. For example, detections at the dam or any other detection array after a fish had already been detected at an array farther downstream resulted in a fish's entire detection history being flagged for manual inspection. The travel time and geographic chronology criterion were effective in identifying noise records that passed other criteria. Ten percent of the remaining fish whose collective detection histories had not been automatically flagged for manually proofing were randomly selected for visual inspection to validate the automated proofing criteria. Lastly, after the fish records selected for manual proofing had been visually inspected, the data were independently reviewed and any interpretive differences in a fish's detection history between the automatic and manual proofing methods were reconciled.

The passage route of each fish was assigned based on the location of its last valid detection at an underwater antenna at the dam. For example, fish last detected in the juvenile fish collection channel were designated to have passed through the bypass, whereas fish last detected at underwater antennas on the ESBS were assigned a turbine passage designator. Passage through spill bays 2 through 8 or through the TSW was assigned similarly. Fish not detected at the dam or last detected in the forebay by aerial antennas in the last 5 min of a fish's history were assigned an "unknown" passage route.

These fish were right-censored at the last known forebay detection time (forebay passage was assumed to occur after the time period in question) for forebay residence time analyses. Fish categorized as transported by barge ($N = 2$) or that entered ODFW's subsample ($N = 39$) after passing through the bypass were right-censored from the dataset after passage.

Spill Periods and Environmental Conditions

No spill treatments were planned in 2009 at Little Goose Dam, so data were divided into spring and summer study periods. A constant 30% spill was maintained throughout the study periods using a modified-uniform spill pattern. Project discharge, total dissolved gas, and water temperature data were summarized for spring and summer study periods to document the environmental conditions that juvenile salmonids experienced during their out-migration. USACE supplied 5-minute dam operation data. Water elevation (NGVD 29) was reported in feet and discharge as thousand cubic feet per second per local convention. Mean project, spillway, TSW, and turbine discharge was summarized for daily, hourly, and diel periods during the spring and summer study periods. Mean daily discharge during the study period for the past 10 years was calculated to characterize the spring and summer studies in the context of previous years. Total dissolved gas and water temperature data measured in the forebay and tailrace were obtained from the University of Washington Columbia Basin Research website (*http://www.cbr.washington.edu/dart/dart.html*) as hourly records.

Fish Data

To describe the fish we radio-tagged and released, we obtained data describing run-of-the-river fish passing through Little Goose Dam. We obtained daily fish passage numbers and the mortality rates in the bypass from the Fish Passage Center (http://*www.fpc.org*). Fork length and weight data recorded daily from the subsampled fish by ODFW also were obtained from the Fish Passage Center.

Approach Distributions and Travel Times

We analyzed behavioral data during overall and by diel periods. Day and night periods were assigned based on civil twilight for each day during the study period (U.S. Naval Oceanography Portal website: http://www.usno.navy.mil/USNO/astronomical-applications/data-services). Diel periods were assigned at first entrance in the forebay for forebay residence time and TSW discovery and entrance efficiency analyses. Approach analyses assigned diel periods when fish were first detected at the site. The egress analysis assigned diel periods at passage. When calculating passage effectiveness and examining the relation between fish passage metrics and water discharged through the dam, we used discharge ($ft^3/s \times 1,000$, thousand cubic feet per second).

To examine the behavior of juvenile salmonids approaching Little Goose Dam, we constructed spatial and temporal approach distributions. Spatial approach distributions were calculated as the percentage of fish first detected among aerial antenna arrays as they entered the forebay and arrived at the dam. The time of first detection by aerial antennas at the forebay entrance and by aerial antennas along the face of the dam were used for temporal approach distributions. We also examined the first detection at each spill bay based on the underwater antennas on the pier noses.

Travel times of radio-tagged fish were calculated to understand how environmental conditions and operations at Little Goose Dam affected the migration timing of juvenile salmonids. Travel times from release near the Central Ferry State Park to the dam were calculated as the elapsed time from release to the first detection by aerial antennas at the forebay entrance. Forebay residence times were calculated as the elapsed time between the first detection by aerial antennas at the forebay entrance and the time of dam passage as determined by underwater antennas.

Egress times were calculated from passage to first detection at the exit site 1.4 km downstream of Little Goose Dam. Only fish with known passage locations and detection at the exit site were included in the analysis. Fish passing through the bypass were excluded, as their entry into the river in the tailrace was downstream of fish passing through the spillway, TSW, or turbine. Fish were designated as entrained in the north shore eddy if they were detected on either the receiver in the northeast corner of the eddy or the receiver located 193 m downstream of the earthen dam on the north shore. Range testing confirmed the fish detected on these two receivers were within the north shore tailrace eddy. Two detection arrays also were installed near the south shore tailrace eddy downstream of the powerhouse, but they were not an effective means for assigning fish presence there because of the noisy environment and our avoidance of the area used heavily by fishermen, so these two detection arrays will not be discussed further in this report.

Forebay Residence Time and Tailrace Egress Time

Patterns in the rate of passage through the spillway, TSW, bypass, and turbines and egress through the tailrace after passage were assessed using time-to-event analyses. This analysis type also was used for measuring the effect of the trash/shear boom on residence time. One of the primary advantages of this type of analysis is the ability to compare passage events over time, rather than a single point in time (for example, the median forebay residence time, tailrace egress time; see Castro-Santos and Haro, 2003). In these analyses, day and night were assigned based on civil twilight for each day during the study period. The analyses were based on fish detected at the forebay entrance array 2 km upstream of the dam, detected on the aerial arrays on the dam (ranges were 200 m upstream of the dam in the spring and 150 m in the summer), and detected by the underwater antennas on the face of the dam (6 m upstream of the dam). Data were right-censored (the event was assumed to occur after the time period in question) at each change of diel period. Two parameters were of primary interest in these analyses: the Kaplan-Meier survivorship function (describing the timing of passage) and the hazard function (describing the rate of passage).

The survivorship function was used to compare the distributions of passage times between passage routes, diel periods, and species. The survivorship function of a variable T is defined as

$$S(t) = \Pr\{T > t\} \tag{1}$$

where T is a random variable with a probability distribution, denoting an event time for an individual. If the event of interest is passing a dam, the survivorship function gives the probability of not passing the dam after time t. As such, the median time occurs when the survivorship function equals 0.5. In the absence of censoring, the survivorship function represents the proportion of the population that has not experienced an event (for example, passing the dam). Survivorship functions were estimated using the Kaplan-Meier method, in which the time-interval boundaries are determined by the event times and censored observations are assumed to be at risk for the entire event period. The alternative is the Life Table method, in which the time interval boundaries can be specified by the analyst and censored data are censored at the midpoint of the time interval (Hosmer and Lemeshow, 1999). Examining the survivorship function can be useful in describing the timing of fish passage as well as the proportion of the population still at risk of passage at different points in time.

The hazard function is defined as

$$h(t) = \lim_{\Delta t \to 0} \Pr\{t \leq T < t + 1 \mid T \geq t\}/ \Delta t \qquad (2)$$

and represents the instantaneous risk, or rate, of an event occurring at time t. The eq. 2 describes a conditional rate: it is the probability of the event occurring in a limited time interval, conditional on the event having not occurred yet,' divided by the length of the interval (which makes it a rate, not a probability; Allison, 1995). A more intuitive definition is the relative rate of an event. For example, in the case of dam passage through one of several possible routes, if the instantaneous hazard of route A is 0.1 and the units of time are hours, it means the instantaneous rate of passage through route A is 10% of the population per hour. Hazards represent risks of individuals, but one can surmise that if the hazard rate of one route is twice that of another, one may expect twice the proportion of fish to pass through route A than through route B during the time in question. We compared hazards to indicate patterns in the rate of passage through various routes over the course of a fish's residence time in the forebay. Hazards are independent of the size of the population and the sum of hazards for individual routes is an estimate of the overall rate of dam passage at any point in time. The reciprocal of the hazard is the expected time for fish to pass the dam if the current instantaneous hazard rate were maintained through time. The counting-process-style data input was used to divide the data into diel period (day or night) and discharge for Cox regression (Hosmer and Lemeshow, 1999). We tested for differences between passage routes or diel periods using the Wilcoxon test. We tested differences between diel periods of passage using Cox proportional hazards regressions analysis.

Behavior Near the Trash/Shear Boom

The trash/shear boom array consisted of 20 sections with one underwater antenna installed per section. Pairs of sections were combined to produce 10 segments of 2 sections each. Because the detection of a fish on a given segment could have been anywhere along the length of the segment, distance from the dam was represented as a range from the start of the segment to the end of the segment (segment 1, 12–36 m; segment 2, 37–60 m; etc.). Further, for estimating distance traveled, the midpoint distance from the dam was used for each segment (segment 1, 24 m; segment 2, 48 m; etc.). Segments were further combined into four segments of 48 m to increase sample sizes for a more generalized representation of behavioral measure. The boom attachment frame was monitored and used for distance traveled estimates, but not included in presence and absence metrics due to overlap with TSW antennas, potential bias due to dissimilar structural features, and antenna type and deployment.

Fish behavior for detection near the trash/shear boom was determined by presence or absence on the boom array. The segment of arrival on the boom was based on first contact with the boom. Direct guidance was defined as individual fish displaying contacts on multiple segments within a 5 min interval. Subsequent contacts in intervals greater than 5 min were defined as indirect guidance, as there was a potential for the individual to have traveled away from the boom and the next contact was actually a re-contact. Net displacement was defined as the difference in distance between the segment of first detection and the segment of last detection for a direct guidance event. Net displacement toward the dam was considered positive, whereas net displacement away from the dam was negative. Only the first direct guidance event was used to determine net displacement and direction of movement. Finally, presence or absence near the boom was used to characterize potential variation in forebay residence time and passage fate.

Estimating Passage and Survival Parameters

Detection and entrance efficiencies were estimated at the TSW. Detection efficiency is the number of fish detected on the underwater antennas within 6 m of the TSW divided by the number of fish detected anywhere in the forebay. Entrance efficiency is the number of fish that passed through the TSW divided by the number of fish detected on the underwater antennas within 6 m of the TSW. Diel periods were assigned at the first detection in the forebay for both the detection efficiency and passage efficiency metrics.

Passage and survival parameters for yearling and subyearling Chinook salmon and juvenile steelhead were estimated using the Route-Specific Survival Model (RSSM; Skalski and others, 2002). The foundation of RSSM is based on the classic Cormack-Jolly-Seber (CJS) single release-recapture models (Cormack 1964, Jolly 1965, and Seber 1965) and the paired release-recapture model of Burnham and others (1987). The RSSM partitions passage and survival parameters among reservoir and route-specific components (table 4; fig. 8). Passage probabilities are estimated using a branching process to estimate conditional probabilities of passing through each route (table 5; fig. 8).

We used the User Specified Estimation Routine (USER, version 4.4.1, Columbia Basin Research, School of Aquatic and Fishery Science, University of Washington, Seattle, Washington) software program to implement the RSSM and estimate passage and survival parameters for the day and night periods (Lady and Skalski, 2009). Detection and passage data for each fish were used to create a numerically coded detection history composed of six digits indicating

1. the release site (1 = upstream, 0 = tailrace);
2. whether fish were detected at the forebay entrance site (1 = detected, 0 = not detected);
3. the route of passage for each fish coded by numbers (2 = spillway, 3 = TSW, 4 = bypass, 5 = turbines); and
4. whether fish were detected at each of the three downstream arrays (1 = detected, 0 = not detected).

For example, the detection history 104101 indicates a fish that was released upstream of the dam (first digit), not detected at the forebay entrance array (second digit), detected within the bypass (third digit), and then the last three digits indicate detection at the first and third downstream arrays, but was not detected at the second downstream array.

Summarized detection histories (appendix C) make up the basic input for the mark-recapture model and are used in the estimation procedure. In general, the survival and detection probabilities are estimated by (1) estimating the probability of each possible detection history from the number of fish with that detection history (that is, from the observed frequencies of each detection history), and (2) using maximum likelihood methods to find parameter estimates of survival, passage, and detection probabilities that are most likely, given the observed data set of detection histories. The RSSM uses a primary likelihood to estimate survival and passage probabilities and auxiliary likelihoods to estimate independent route-specific detection probabilities.

Table 4. Definition of passage, survival, and detection parameters estimated by the route-specific survival model (maximum likelihood estimates, MLE) or derived as functions of MLEs for juvenile salmonids passing Little Goose Dam, during spring and summer 2009.

Parameter	Source	Definition
Day	MLE	Probability of passing the dam during daylight hours.
Night	Derived	Probability of passing the dam during non-daylight hours (1- day).
SP	MLE	Probability of passing through the spillway (spill bays 2–8 + TSW).
SB	MLE	Probability of passing through spill bays 2–8 given that a fish was passing through the spillway.
BYP	MLE	Probability of passing through the bypass given that a fish was passing through the powerhouse.
Pr bays 2–8, *Pr* tsw, *Pr* byp, *Pr* tur	Derived	Probability of passage through spill bays 2–8, TSW, bypass, or turbines.
Pr bays 1–8	Derived	Probability of combined spillway passage, spill bays 1–8.
Pr byp+tur	Derived	Probability of combined powerhouse passage.
FGE	Derived	Fish Guidance Efficiency. Proportion of fish that enter a turbine intake and are subsequently guided by screens into the bypass divided by the total number of fish passing into the turbine intake.
FPE	Derived	Fish Passage Efficiency. Proportion of fish passing a dam through any non-turbine route divided by the total number of fish passing the dam through all available routes.
SPE	Derived	Spill Passage Efficiency. Proportion of fish passing a dam through spill bays 2-8 divided by the total number of fish passing the dam through all available routes.
SPS bays 2–8	Derived	Spill Passage Effectiveness. Ratio of the proportion of fish passing through spill bays 2–8 to the proportion of total water volume at the dam discharged through spill bays 2–8.
SOS	Derived	Surface Outlet Effectiveness. Ratio of the proportion of fish passing through the TSW to the proportion of total water volume at the dam discharged through the TSW.
SPS	Derived	Combined spill bay and TSW Passage Effectiveness. Ratio of the proportion of fish passing through spill bays 1–8 combined to the proportion of total water volume at the dam discharged through spill bays 1–8 combined.
P fb	MLE	Detection probability of the forebay entrance site.
P sp1, *P* tsw1, *P* byp1, *P* tur1	MLE	Detection probability of the first array (underwater antennas) on the spillway, TSW, bypass, or turbine.
P sp2, *P* tsw2, *P* byp2, *P* tur2	MLE	Detection probability of the second array (underwater antennas) on the spillway, TSW, bypass, or turbine.
P sp, *P* tsw, *P* byp, *P* tur	Derived	Overall detection probability of the arrays on the spillway, TSW, bypass, or turbine.
P concrete	Derived	Overall detection probability at the dam (that is, average detection probability for all routes weighted by the proportion of fish passing each route).
*Pd*1 sp, *Pd*1 tsw, *Pd*1 byp, *Pd*1 tur, *Pd*1 con	MLE	Detection probability of the first downstream detection array downstream of Little Goose Dam for fish passing through spill bays 2–8, TSW, bypass, and turbines, or control fish released immediately downstream of the dam in the tailrace.
*S*1 sp, *S*1 tsw, *S*1 byp, *S*1 tur	MLE	Single-release survival estimate from detection in spill bays 2–8, TSW, bypass, or turbines to the first downstream detection array downstream of Little Goose Dam.
*S*1 con	MLE	Single-release survival estimate from the point of release of the control fish in the tailrace to the first downstream detection array.

Pd2 sp, Pd2 tsw, Pd2 byp, Pd2 tur, Pd2 con	MLE	Detection probability of the second downstream detection array downstream of Little Goose Dam for fish passing through spill bays 2–8, TSW, bypass, and turbines, or control fish released immediately downstream of the dam in the tailrace.
S2 sp, S2 tsw, S2 byp, S2 tur, S2 con	MLE	Single-release survival estimate for the reach between the first and second downstream detection arrays for fish detected passing through spill bays 2–8, TSW, bypass, or turbines, and control fish released in the tailrace of Little Goose Dam.
λ sp, λ tsw, λ byp, λ tur, λ con	MLE	Joint probability of surviving the reach between the 2nd and 3rd detection arrays downstream of Little Goose Dam and being detected for fish passing through the spill bays, TSW, bypass, or turbines.
S fb	MLE	Survival probability from point of detection at forebay entrance site to the point of detection within passage routes at Little Goose Dam.
S bays 2–8, S TSW, S bays 1–8, S byp, S tur, S powerhouse	Derived	Relative survival probability from detection in spill bays 2–8, TSW, spill bays 2–8 and TSW, bypass, turbines, or bypass + turbines to the point of release of control groups of fish in tailrace.
S concrete	Derived	Average survival probability of dam passage through all routes weighted by the probability of passing each route.
S dam	Derived	Joint survival probability of S fb and S concrete.

Each unique detection history has a probability of occurrence that can be expressed in terms of the probabilities of the survival, passage, and detection probability parameters (appendix C). For example, consider the individual fish history described above (fish history: 104101). The probability of this fish history is the joint probability that it survived through the reservoir (S pool), survived through the forebay undetected ((1-P fb)*S fb), passed into the bypass ((1-SP)*BYP), was detected in the bypass (P byp), survived through the bypass and first reach downstream of the dam and was detected at the first downstream detection array (S1 byp*Pd1 byp), survived through the second reach downstream of the dam undetected (S2 byp*(1-Pd2 byp)), and survived the third downstream reach and was detected at the last downstream array (λ). Thus, the probability of detection history 104101 can be written as

S pool*(1-P fb)*S fb*(1-SP)*BYP*P byp*S1 byp*Pd1 byp*S2 byp*(1-Pd2 byp)*λ.

The expected probability of each detection history is then estimated from the observed frequencies of fish with that detection history. Given the expected probability of each detection history and its probability function in terms of survival, passage, and detection probabilities (appendix C), likelihood methods were used to find the combination of survival, passage, and detection probabilities that were most likely to occur, given the dataset of observed detection histories. The maximum likelihood function is simply the joint probability of all possible detection histories. Sampling variances for parameters estimated by maximum likelihood were calculated using the inverse Hessian matrix provided by the USER software. Further details on the maximum likelihood methods for estimating survival and detection probabilities, including estimation of theoretical variances, can be found in Burnham and others (1987), Lebreton and others (1992), and Skalski and others (2001).

After estimating model parameters using maximum likelihood methods, route-specific relative survival estimates and other additional parameters were estimated as functions of model parameters (table 5). Variances for these parameters were calculated using the Delta method (Seber, 1982). Ninety-five percent confidence intervals for all model parameters were calculated using profile likelihood methods as supplied in USER software.

All fish were assigned to diel time periods based as closely as possible on their time of passage at Little Goose Dam. Generally, time of passage was assigned to the last detection of fish on underwater detection arrays in each of the passage routes. If fish were not detected in a passage route, they were assigned a diel period based on (1) the time of their last detection at the dam, (2) the time of their last detection at the forebay entrance site, or (3) the time of their first detection by telemetry arrays in the tailrace. Lastly, fish not detected at the dam, forebay, or tailrace were assigned to a day or night period in the same proportions as the fish that were detected at the time of passage. Overall passage and survival estimates were derived by averaging the day and night estimates weighted by the proportion of tagged fish passing during the day and night periods.

Initial model outputs indicated that more fish were detected at downstream detection arrays than would be expected given the route-specific detection probabilities estimated from the double arrays in each passage route. These numbers were not large (yearling Chinook salmon, $N = 7$; juvenile steelhead, $N = 10$; subyearling Chinook salmon, $N = 36$), but nonetheless resulted in some residuals between 3 and 8. This suggested there were potentially small zone(s) within one or more passage routes with poor or no coverage by the telemetry arrays. Model fit was improved by comparing models with various detection scenarios that assumed a particular route(s) was suspect and by estimating the detection probability for the route(s) using the primary likelihood instead of the double array. The models were ranked using Akaike's Information Criterion (AIC) and the model with the lowest AIC was selected (Burnham and Anderson, 2002). Although this resulted in better fitting models for each species, the effect was negligible on passage and survival estimates because the detection probabilities for all passage routes were high. Once the best model for the route-specific detection probabilities was selected, models were compared sequentially that assumed that the survival or the detection probabilities within downstream reaches 2 and 3, and the detection probabilities for downstream array 1, were either equal or not equal (for example, S2 sp=S2 tsw=S2 byp=S2 tur vs. S2 sp≠S2 tsw≠S2 byp≠S2 tur) to determine the most efficient model for each species.

Significant statistical differences in route-specific survival and passage between diel periods were determined by estimating these differences as functions of the model parameters and constructing 95% profile-likelihood intervals around the estimated differences. If the confidence interval for the estimated difference did not include 0, the difference was considered significant at the $\alpha = 0.5$ level.

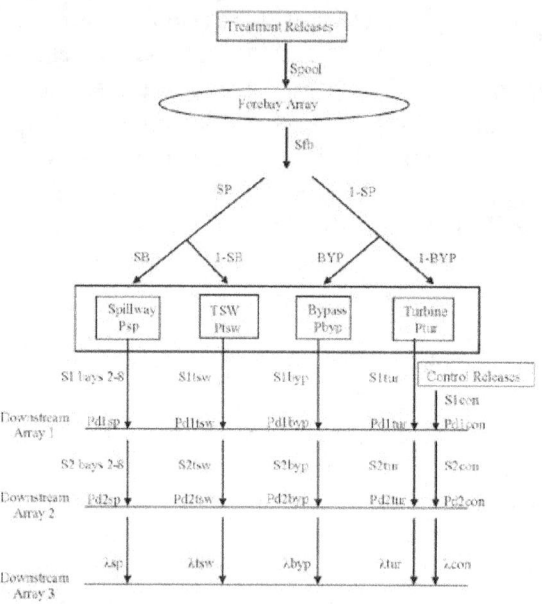

Figure 8. Schematic of the route-specific survival model of juvenile salmonids passing Little Goose Dam during 2009. Shown are fish releases and passage, detection, and survival probabilities. See table 4 for the parameter definitions.

Table 5. Equations for parameters estimated as functions of maximum likelihood estimates for the route-specific survival model, Little Goose Dam, 2009.

[Parameter definitions are shown in table 4]

Parameter	Equation
Pr bays 2–8	SP*SB
Pr tsw	SP*(1-SB)
Pr bays 1–8	*Pr* bays 2–8+*Pr* tsw
Pr byp	(1-SP)*(BYP)
Pr tur	(1-SP)*(1-BYP)
Pr powerhouse	*Pr* byp+*Pr* tur
P sp	1-(1-*P* sp1)*(1-*P* sp2)
P tsw	1-(1-*P* tsw1)*(1-*P* tsw2)
P byp	1-(1-*P* byp1)*(1-*P* byp2)
P tur	1-(1-*P* tur1)*(1-*P* tur2)
P concrete	(*P* sp**Pr* bays 2–8)+(*P* tsw**Pr* tsw)+(*P* byp**Pr* byp)+(*P* tur**Pr* tur)
SPS bays 2–8	*Pr* bays 2–8/proportion of total water volume spilled through spill bays 2–8
SOS	*Pr* tsw/proportion of total water volume passed through the TSW
SPS bays 1–8	*Pr* bays1–8/proportion total water volume passed through the spillway
FGE	*Pr* byp/(*Pr* byp+*Pr* tur)
FPE	*Pr* bays 2–8+*Pr* tsw+*Pr* byp
S sp (bays 2–8)	*S*1 sp/ *S*1con
S tsw	*S*1 tsw/ *S*1con
S bays 1–8	*S* sp + *S* tsw
S byp	*S* byp/ *S*1con
S tur	*S* tur/ *S*1con
S powerhouse	*S* byp + *S* tur
S dam	*S* fb*(*S* sp**Pr* sp)+(*S* tsw**Pr* tsw)+(*S* byp**Pr* byp)+(*S* tur**Pr* tur)
S concrete	(*S* bays 2–8**Pr* bays 2–8)+(*S* tsw**Pr* tsw)+(*S* byp**Pr* byp)+(*S* tur**Pr* tur)

Survival and detection probabilities from the RSSM model are subject to 11 assumptions. The first seven of these assumptions relate to inferences to the population of interest, error in interpreting radio signals, and statistical fit of the data to the model's structure:

1. Tagged individuals are representative of the population of interest. For example, if the target population is subyearling Chinook salmon, then the sample of tagged fish should be drawn from that population.

2. Survival probabilities of tagged fish are the same as that of untagged fish. For example, the tagging procedures or detection of fish at downstream telemetry arrays should not influence survival or detection probabilities. If the tag negatively affects survival, then single-reach estimates of survival rates will be biased accordingly.

3. All sampling (that is, detection) events are instantaneous. That is, sampling should take place over a short distance relative to the distance between telemetry arrays so that the chance of mortality at a telemetry array is minimized. This assumption is necessary to attribute mortality correctly to a specific river reach. This assumption usually is satisfied by the location of telemetry arrays and the downstream migration rates of juvenile salmonids.

4. Survival or mortality of one fish has no effect on survival or mortality of other fish.

5. The prior detection history of a tagged fish has no effect on its subsequent survival. This assumption could be violated if there are portions of the river that are not monitored for tagged fish. For example, for PIT-tagged fish, some fish may repeatedly pass through bypasses where PIT-tag readers are located, whereas other fish may consistently pass through spillways, which are not monitored. If fish passing through these routes have different survival rates, then this assumption could be violated. This assumption should be satisfied in the current radio telemetry study by the passive nature of detecting radio tags, by monitoring all routes of passage at Little Goose Dam, and by monitoring the entire width of the river at downstream detection arrays.

6. All tagged fish alive at a sampling location have the same detection probability. This assumption should be met during the study by monitoring the entire width of the channel for the radio-tagged fish.

7. All tags are correctly identified and the status of tagged fish (that is, alive or dead) is known without error. This assumes fish do not lose their tags and that the tag is functioning when the fish is in the study area. Additionally, this assumes that all detections are of live fish and that dead fish are not detected and interpreted as live (that is, false positive detections).

8. Survival in the lower river segments is conditionally independent of survival in the upper river segments

9. Survival is equal for treatment and control releases (see fig. 8) between the release point of control fish and the first downstream telemetry array. Because of the short nature of the study period, small size of the study area, and the frequency and timing of the upstream and tailrace releases, adequate mixing should have been achieved to meet this assumption and assumption #8.

10. The two detection arrays within each route are independent. This assumption is necessary to obtain valid estimates of route-specific detection probabilities. To fulfill this assumption, fish detected in one array should have the same probability of detection in the second array compared to fish not detected in the first array.

11. Passage routes of radio-tagged fish are known without error. This assumption is important to avoid bias in passage and survival probabilities.

Assumptions #2, #6, and #7 were formally examined to test for differences in survival of tagged fish among taggers, false-positive detections, and to ensure that tags did not fail prior to fish exiting the study area. The question of potential bias in survival estimates because of differences among taggers was examined by creating separate treatment and control fish likelihoods for each individual tagger in a single RSSM model. Two versions of these models were created for each species, one version hypothesized that survival probabilities for a given reach were the same among taggers and the second version of the model hypothesized that the survival probabilities differed among taggers. The two competing models for each survival reach were ranked using AIC to see which assumption was best supported by the data. When differences among taggers were suggested, individual point estimates and profile-likelihood confidence intervals were examined to determine the nature of the differences. To address the question of false positive detections, a subsample of euthanized tagged fish was released in the tailrace to determine if they were detected at the downstream survival gates (described in section, "Fish Releases"). To address the question of tag failure prior to a fish exiting the study area, a controlled tag-life study was done to estimate the probability of tag failure at any point in time after tags were turned on. The methods of Townsend and others (2006) then were used to estimate the average probability that a tag was alive when fish were in the study area (described in appendix B).

Results

Spring Migration Period

Dam Operations and Environmental Conditions

There were no planned treatments at Little Goose Dam in 2009, so operations consisted of 30% spill and use of the TSW at the low crest elevation during ambient conditions. The spring study period was from April 18 to June 5, 2009, and the summer study period was from June 6 to July 6, 2009. In comparison to the previous 10 years, the daily discharge represented an above average year. Specifically, the mean daily discharge for spring 2009 was the third highest with only 1999 and 2006 having a higher mean daily discharge (fig. 9). Mean daily total discharge during the spring study period was 111.6 thousand ft^3/s ranging from 60.9 to164.9 thousand ft^3/s. Discharge was similar during day and night periods, with averages of 111.9 thousand ft^3/s during the day and 111.2 thousand ft^3/s during the night. The mean daily total discharge for TSW was 11.1 thousand ft^3/s, ranging from 10.5 to 12.0 thousand ft^3/s (fig. 10, appendix D). There was little variation of the percentage of discharge of the powerhouse and spillway for either diel period. During the day, the powerhouse discharged 71.6%, the spillway discharged 18.7% and the TSW discharged 9.7% of the total water through the dam (28.4% for total spillway; fig. 11). During the night, the discharge percentages for powerhouse, spillway, and TSW were 71.4, 18.6, and 10.0%, respectively (28.6% for total spillway; fig. 11).

Environmental conditions generally were similar to those from the previous 10 years. Forebay elevations and water temperatures during the spring study period were similar to their 10-year averages. The mean forebay elevation was 193.1 m (633.4 ft; NGVD 29) (range = 192.9–193.3 m) and daily forebay temperature increased steadily from 8.1 °C at the beginning of the season to 13.0 °C at the end of the season (appendix D). The mean total dissolved gas during spring 2009 was 110.8% with a range between 104.1 and 126.1% compared to a mean of 108.9% and a range of 106.2 to 113.8% over the last 10 years (appendix D).

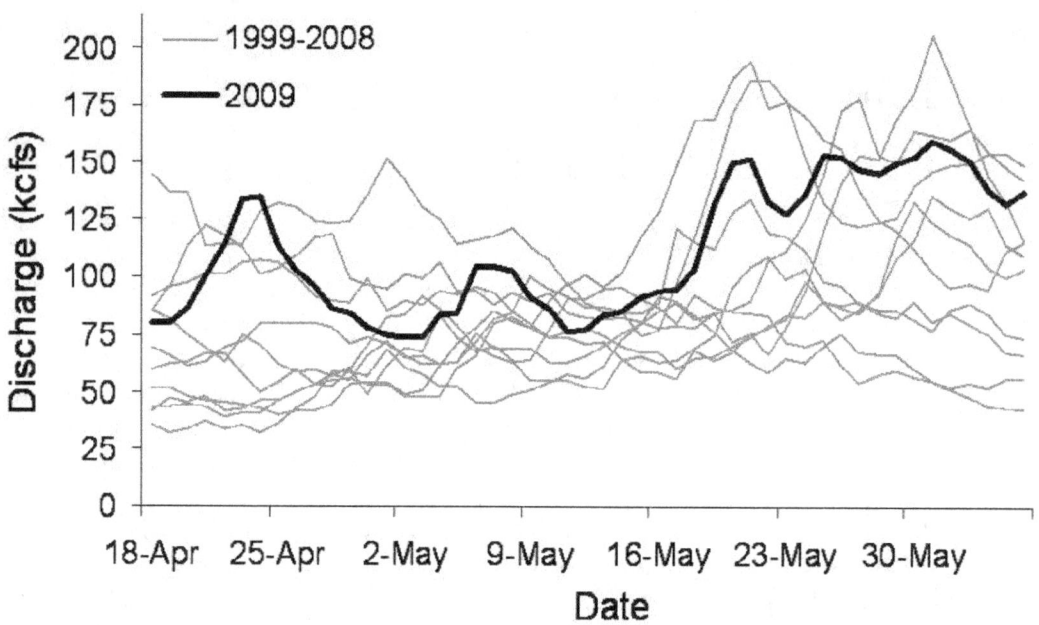

Figure 9. Hydrograph showing total daily project discharge at Little Goose Dam during the spring study period (April 18 to June 5) for the previous 10 years (1999–2008) and current year (2009).

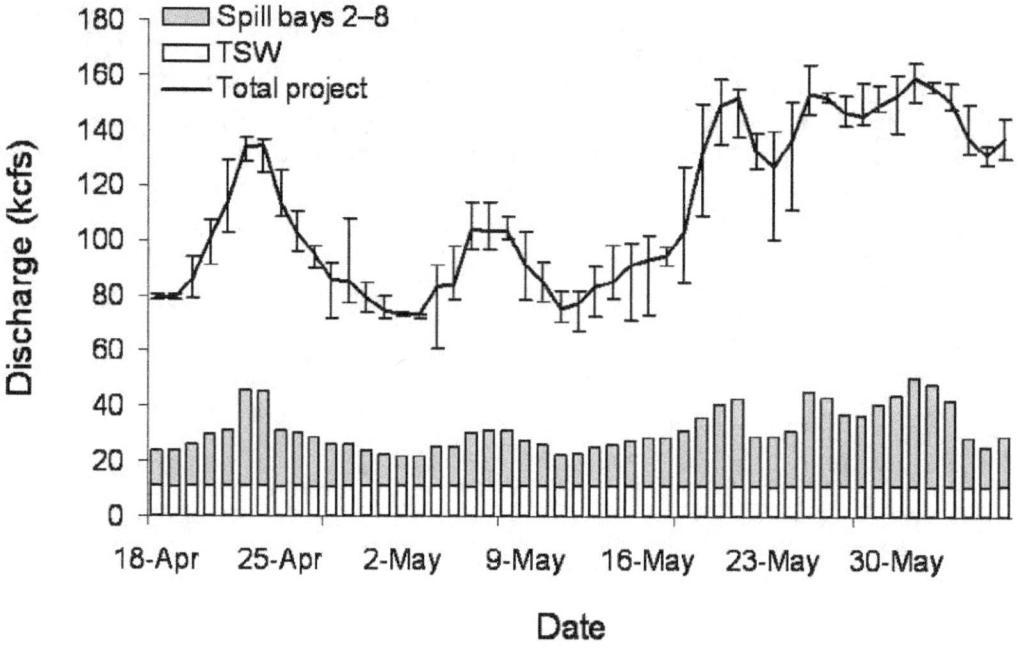

Figure 10. Hydrograph showing mean daily total project discharge, TSW discharge (bay 1), and conventional spill bays discharge (bays 2–8), through Little Goose Dam during the spring study period April 18 to June 5, 2009. Whisker bars represent the minimum and maximum discharge for each day.

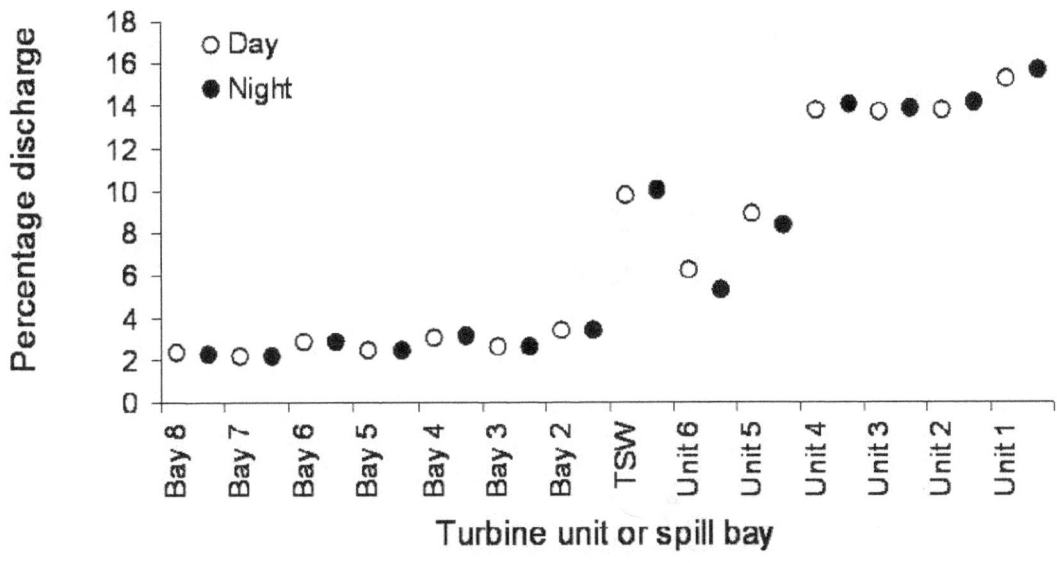

Figure 11. Hydrograph showing percentage of total discharge through each turbine unit or spill bay by diel period at Little Goose Dam during the spring study period (April 18 to June 5, 2009).

Tagging and Releasing Fish

The average size of radio-tagged yearling Chinook salmon and juvenile steelhead was comparable to fish sampled at the juvenile fish facility (fig. 12). No significant difference was found between fish weights of the control and treatment groups for yearling Chinook salmon ($t = 0.26$, df = 1,344, $P = 0.80$) or for juvenile steelhead ($t = -0.22$, df = 1,383, $P = 0.82$; table 6). Eighty-seven percent of yearling Chinook salmon and 100% of juvenile steelhead collected at the Little Goose Dam juvenile fish bypass facility during the study period were 14.2 g or larger, the minimum size fish to maintain a tag weight to body weight ratio of about 5%. Summaries of fish sizes and release are shown in appendix A.

The study period encompassed a large proportion of the run timing of juvenile spring migrants. For yearling Chinook salmon, the run percentile was just more than 2% when our study started and 99% when it ended, representing 97% of the run. For juvenile steelhead, the run percentile was less than 1% when the study began and 96% when it ended, representing 95% of the run (fig. 13).

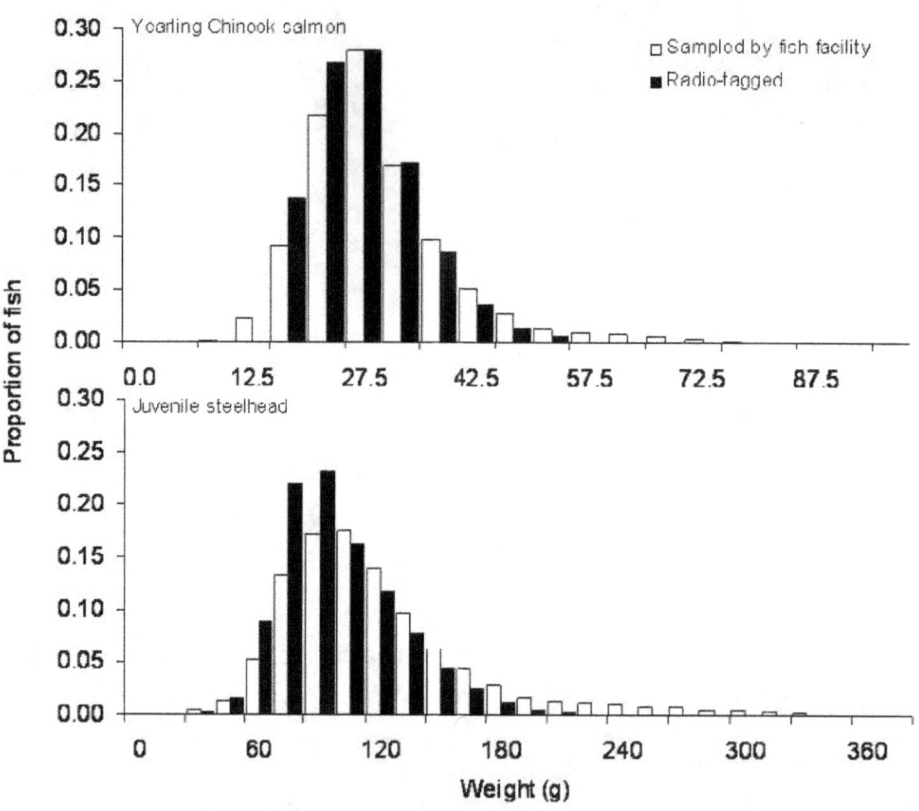

Figure 12. Graphs showing frequency distributions of weight of yearling Chinook salmon and juvenile steelhead collected at the Little Goose juvenile fish facility compared to the frequency distribution of fish radio-tagged during spring 2009. Note the different x-axis scales.

Table 6. Summary statistics of fork length and weight of radio-tagged yearling Chinook salmon and juvenile steelhead released at Little Goose Dam, spring 2009.

[N, number of fish; SD, standard deviation]

Species	Release group	N	Fork Length, in millimeters			Weight, in grams		
			Mean	SD	Range	Mean	SD	Range
Yearling Chinook salmon	Treatment	883	139.3	11.2	115–195	26.7	7.2	14.4–70.3
	Control	587	139.1	11.5	110–226	26.6	7.0	14.3–53.4
	Euthanized	50	136.7	10.7	110–156	25.4	6.3	14.4–39.3
Juvenile steelhead	Treatment	880	214.2	23.5	113–275	90.3	29.2	19.7–205.6
	Control	587	215.1	21.7	112–284	90.1	28.5	14.2–216.4
	Euthanized	50	219.9	22.0	172– 271	96.8	30.0	44.9–173.6

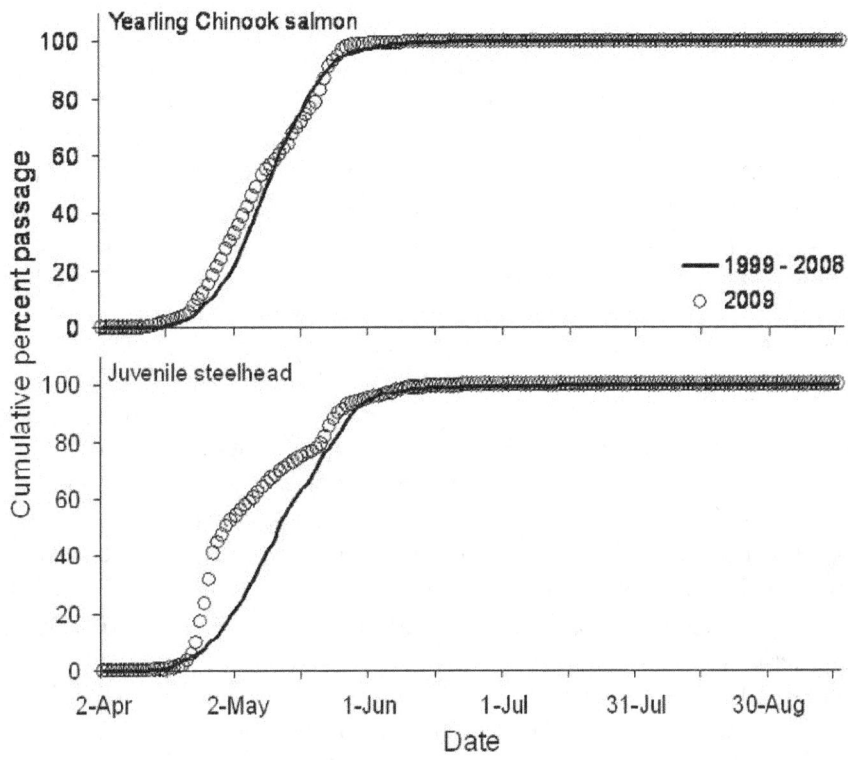

Figure 13. Graphs showing cumulative passage distribution of yearling Chinook salmon and juvenile steelhead at Little Goose Dam. Shown are the historical 10-year average (1999–2008) and the current year (2009). Yearling Chinook salmon data are for hatchery fish except for year 2000 when the data are combined with wild fish. Steelhead data are combined wild and hatchery data for all years. Data provided by the Fish Passage Center (http://*www.fpc.org*).

Mortality rates were low during the post-tagging holding period. From April 17 to May 21, we radio-tagged and released 1,520 (1,470 live and 50 euthanized) yearling Chinook salmon, and 1,517 (1,467 live and 50 euthanized) juvenile steelhead. For yearling Chinook salmon, there was one mortality in the control group (0.16%, 1 of 638) and no mortalities in the treatment group (0 of 883) during the post-tagging holding period. For juvenile steelhead, the mortality rate for the treatment group during the post-tagging holding period was 0.11% (1 of 881) and was not significantly different ($\chi^2 = 1.79$, $P = 0.18$) than the mortality rate of the control group, 0.47% (3 of 640). Tagging mortality rates were within the range of other studies using surgical implantation (Axel and others, 2007; Perry and others, 2007). In comparison, during the same time period, the mortality rate at the Little Goose Dam juvenile fish bypass facility was 0.07% for hatchery yearling Chinook salmon and 0.01% for hatchery juvenile steelhead (Data provided by the Fish Passage Center, www.fpc.org).

Approach Distribution

The location and timing of first detections of yearling Chinook salmon and juvenile steelhead 2 km upstream of the dam were similar. Most fish were first detected at the north shore antenna site (77–80%). Sixty-five percent of yearling Chinook salmon and 78% of juvenile steelhead arrived at the forebay entrance antennas during the day (fig. 14).

As the fish approached to within 200 m from the dam, they were primarily near the earthen dam and spillway. Based on the new earthen dam array, 44% of yearling Chinook salmon were first detected within 200 m of the dam by antennas on the spillway, 36% by antennas on the earthen dam, and 20% by antennas on the powerhouse. First detections of juvenile steelhead on these arrays were similar to those of yearling Chinook salmon, with 50% at the spillway, 27% at the earthen dam, and 23% at the powerhouse (fig. 15).

The difference in range of the old and new earthen dam arrays resulted in slight differences in the areas of first detection. However, the differences were not great enough to alter the conclusion that most fish were first detected within about 200 m from the dam near the earthen dam and spillway. Use of the old earthen dam array resulted in more fish first detected at the earthen dam and fewer at the spillway and powerhouse. When the old earthen dam array was used, 54–61% of the spring migrants were first detected at the earthen dam, 24–29% were first detected on the spillway aerial array, and 15–17% were first detected on the powerhouse aerial array.

The timing and location of arrival within 200 m from the dam was slightly different during day and night periods (fig. 16). Fish from both species approached the dam during all times of the day and night, but arrivals of juvenile steelhead were greater than yearling Chinook salmon in the afternoon and less during the several hours after midnight. During the day and night, yearling Chinook salmon arrived predominantly upstream of the earthen dam and spillway, but the spillway portion was greater during the night than during the day. Most yearling Chinook salmon were first detected near the spillway and earthen dam during the day and night (fig. 16). Juvenile steelhead arrived predominantly at the spillway during the day (52.9%) and in similar percentages at the spillway (41.5%) and powerhouse (38.6%) during the night.

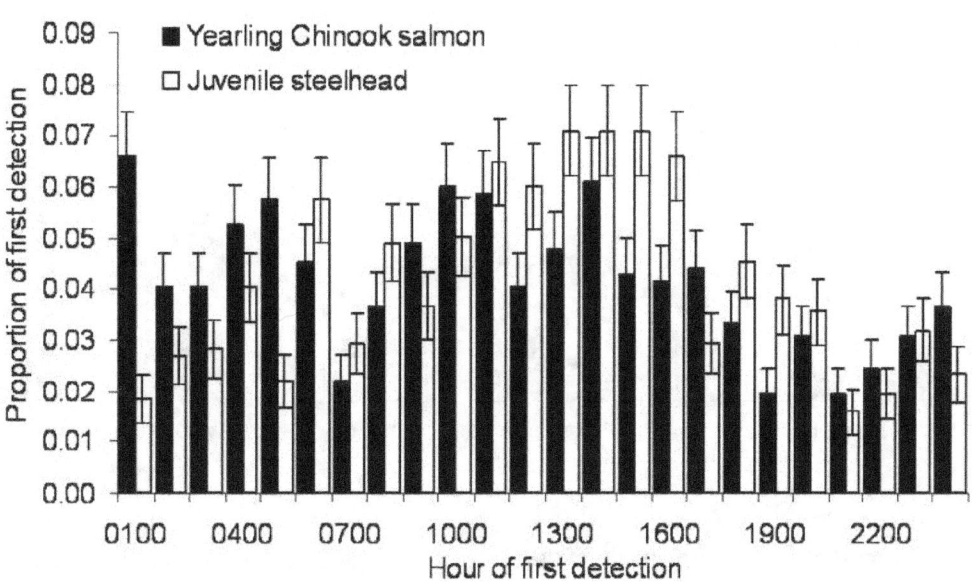

Figure 14. Graph showing proportion of yearling Chinook salmon and juvenile steelhead first detected at the entrance sites (2 km upstream of Little Goose Dam) by hour of arrival, spring 2009. Whisker bars represent the standard error of each hourly proportion. Sample sizes were 818 yearling Chinook salmon and 818 juvenile steelhead.

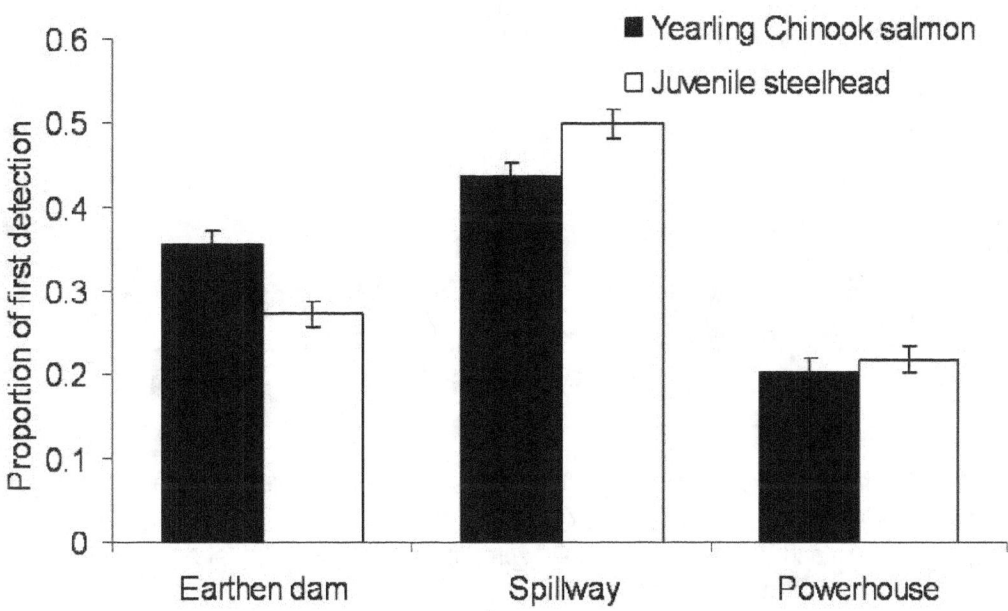

Figure 15. Graph showing approach distribution for proportion of yearling Chinook salmon and juvenile steelhead first detected by aerial antennas using the new earthen dam array, Little Goose Dam, spring 2009. Whisker bars represent the standard error of each hourly proportion. Sample sizes were 799 yearling Chinook salmon and 759 juvenile steelhead.

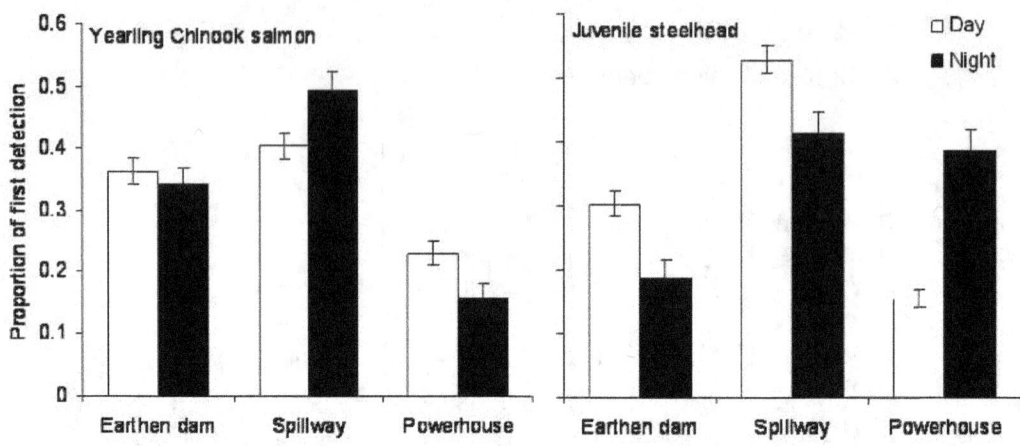

Figure 16. Graph showing proportion of first detection of yearling Chinook salmon and juvenile steelhead arriving within 200 m by diel period, Little Goose Dam, spring 2009. Whisker bars represent the standard error of each hourly proportion. Sample sizes for day and night were 518 and 285 yearling Chinook salmon and 561 and 207 juvenile steelhead, respectively.

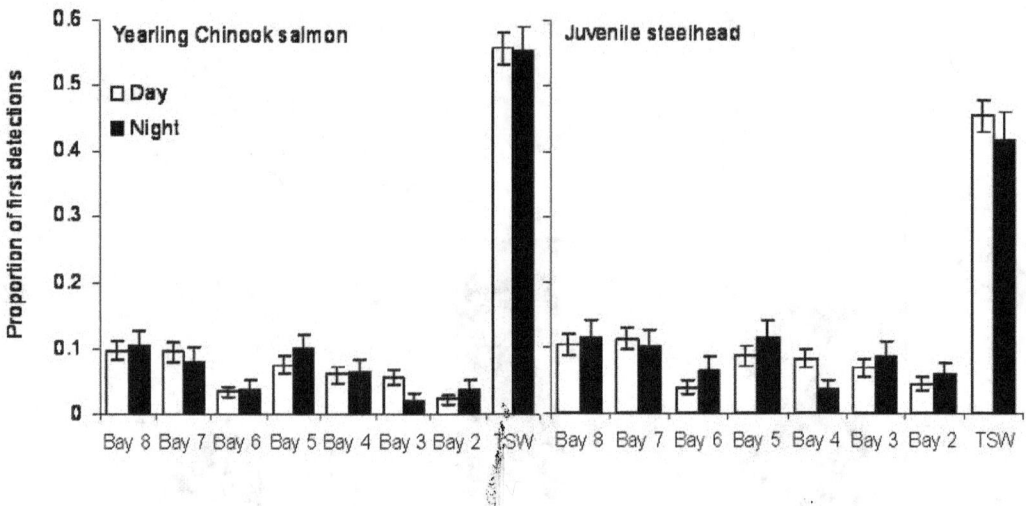

Figure 17. Graph showing proportion of yearling Chinook salmon and juvenile steelhead first detection on spillway underwater antennas by diel period, Little Goose Dam, spring 2009. Whisker bars represent the standard error of each hourly proportion. Sample sizes for day and night were 428 and 183 yearling Chinook salmon and 397 and 137 juvenile steelhead, respectively.

Fish arrivals within 6 m of the spillway were primarily near the TSW in spill bay 1. The location of more than 50% of yearling Chinook salmon and 40% of juvenile steelhead first detected within 6 m of the spillway was near the TSW and fewer than 12% were first detected at any one of the other spill bays (fig. 17). This trend was similar during the day and night. Overall, 76% of yearling Chinook salmon and 70% of juvenile steelhead were first detected within 6 m of the spillway.

Travel Time

Juvenile salmonids traveled from release to the forebay of the dam in about 1 day. The median travel time of yearling Chinook salmon was 29.65 h and ranged from 5.02 to 302.16 h (table 7). The median travel time of juvenile steelhead was 21.62 h and ranged from 2.72 to 330.91 h (table 7).

Table 7. Travel time of radio-tagged yearling Chinook salmon and juvenile steelhead from release near Central Ferry State Park (rkm 134) to first detection at the forebay entrance site (rkm 115; 2 rkm upstream of the dam), Little Goose Dam, spring 2009.

[N, number of fish; Min., minimum; Max, maximum; SD, standard deviation]

Species	N	Travel time, in hours				
		Mean	Median	Min.	Max.	SD
Yearling Chinook salmon	818	34.34	29.65	5.02	302.16	24.87
Juvenile steelhead	818	26.01	21.62	2.72	330.91	17.36

Forebay Residence Time

The forebay residence times of fish arriving in the forebay during the day were similar to those arriving during the night. The median forebay residence time of yearling Chinook salmon was 6.7 h (95% CI 6.2–7.3 h) for those arriving in the forebay during the day and 5.0 h (95% CI 4.5–5.5 h) for those arriving during the night (fig. 18, appendix E). Median forebay residence times of juvenile steelhead arriving in the forebay were 8.4 h (95% CI 7.8–9.0 h) and 5.6 h (95% CI 4.5–6.4 h) during the day and night, respectively (fig. 18, appendix E). The 90th percentiles of passage of yearling Chinook salmon arriving during the day and night were 21.2 and 17.8 h, respectively. The 90th percentiles of passage of juvenile steelhead arriving during the day and night were 25.4 and 24.2 h. Even though the maximum forebay residence times were more than 100 h, less than 6% of yearling Chinook salmon and 11% of juvenile steelhead remained in the forebay 24 h after their arrival (fig. 18, appendix E).

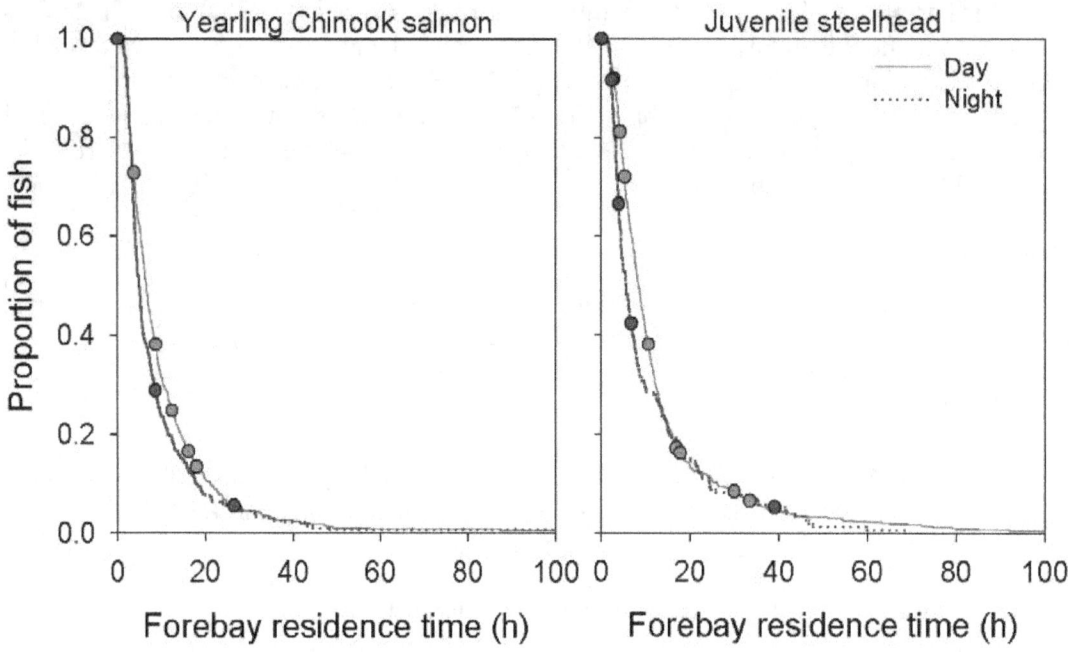

Figure 18. Graphs showing Kaplan-Meier survivorship function (proportion of fish remaining in forebay) of forebay residence time by diel period of yearling Chinook salmon and juvenile steelhead, Little Goose Dam, spring 2009. Circles represent fish detected in the forebay but censored at last forebay detection prior to unknown route of passage.

Forebay residence times did not differ among passage routes when the entire 2-km forebay was considered, but differences in forebay residence times were evident when fish were nearer to the dam. To investigate the potential relation between forebay residence time and route of passage, the forebay was divided into three reaches for analysis: 2 km to 200 m from the dam; 200 m to 6 m from the dam; and 6 m from the dam to passage. In the forebay reach from 2 km to 200 m upstream of the dam, forebay residence times were similar among passage routes (fig. 19). There were no differences between passage routes in this reach for yearling Chinook salmon ($\chi^2 = 6.0$, df = 3, $P = 0.1096$) or juvenile steelhead ($\chi^2 = 4.0$, df = 3, $P = 0.2647$). The median time to pass this 1,800 m reach was 3.3 h (95% CI 3.1–3.5 h) for yearling Chinook salmon when pooling passage routes (fig. 19). The median time for juvenile steelhead to pass this reach was 3.6 h (95% CI 3.3–3.8; fig. 19). Fish passing through turbines resided longer in this reach than those passing the other routes; however, few fish passed through turbines. The residence time for the 90th percentile of passage (proportion remaining in the forebay was 10%) of yearling Chinook salmon was 8.7 and 10.6 h for juvenile steelhead (fig. 19).

38

In the 200 m to 6 m reach, residence times differed among passage routes (yearling Chinook salmon $\chi^2 = 40.1$, df = 3, $P < 0.001$; juvenile steelhead $\chi^2 = 34.9$, df = 3, $P < 0.001$). The median times to transit this 194 m reach were similar for yearling Chinook salmon and juvenile steelhead (0.4–1.7 h depending on the route; fig. 19). The primary differences among routes occurred in the latter 50% of the passage distributions and thus the median residence times were similar among routes in this reach. The residence times for the 90th percentile of passage of yearling Chinook salmon ranged from 2.3 to 13.4 h among routes, with the time to pass the spillway route being shortest, followed by TSW, bypass, and turbines. The residence times for 90th percentile of passage of juvenile steelhead ranged from 4.8 to 8.8 h and the two spillway routes were similar to one another, but shorter than the bypass. Steelhead passing through the turbine had the shortest residence time in this reach; however, very few fish passed through this route.

Differences in reach transit times among routes of passage were most evident within 6 m of passage. In this reach, fish detected near the spillway routes traveled a shorter distance prior to passage than fish passing through the powerhouse routes, so some differences among routes may be expected. This difference is because of the positions of the antennas relative to the passage routes: antennas at spillway routes were on pier noses or within the route itself, whereas those for the powerhouse routes were on the ESBS (radio antennas) and within the juvenile fish bypass system (PIT and radio antennas). Median times to transit this reach typically were several minutes, although some fish, particularly juvenile steelhead, took several hours. The 90th percentile of passage of yearling Chinook salmon was 5.2 h for TSW passage, 0.3 h for spill passage, 8.0 h for bypass passage, and 5.0 h for turbine passage. The 90th percentile of passage of juvenile steelhead was 7.0 h for TSW passage, 10.8 h for spillway passage, 15.9 h for bypass passage, and 8.3 h for turbine passage (fig. 19). Median forebay residence times in the entire 2 km reach were 6.0 h (95% CI 5.6–6.6 h) for yearling Chinook salmon and 7.8 h (95% CI 7.4–8.4 h) for juvenile steelhead.

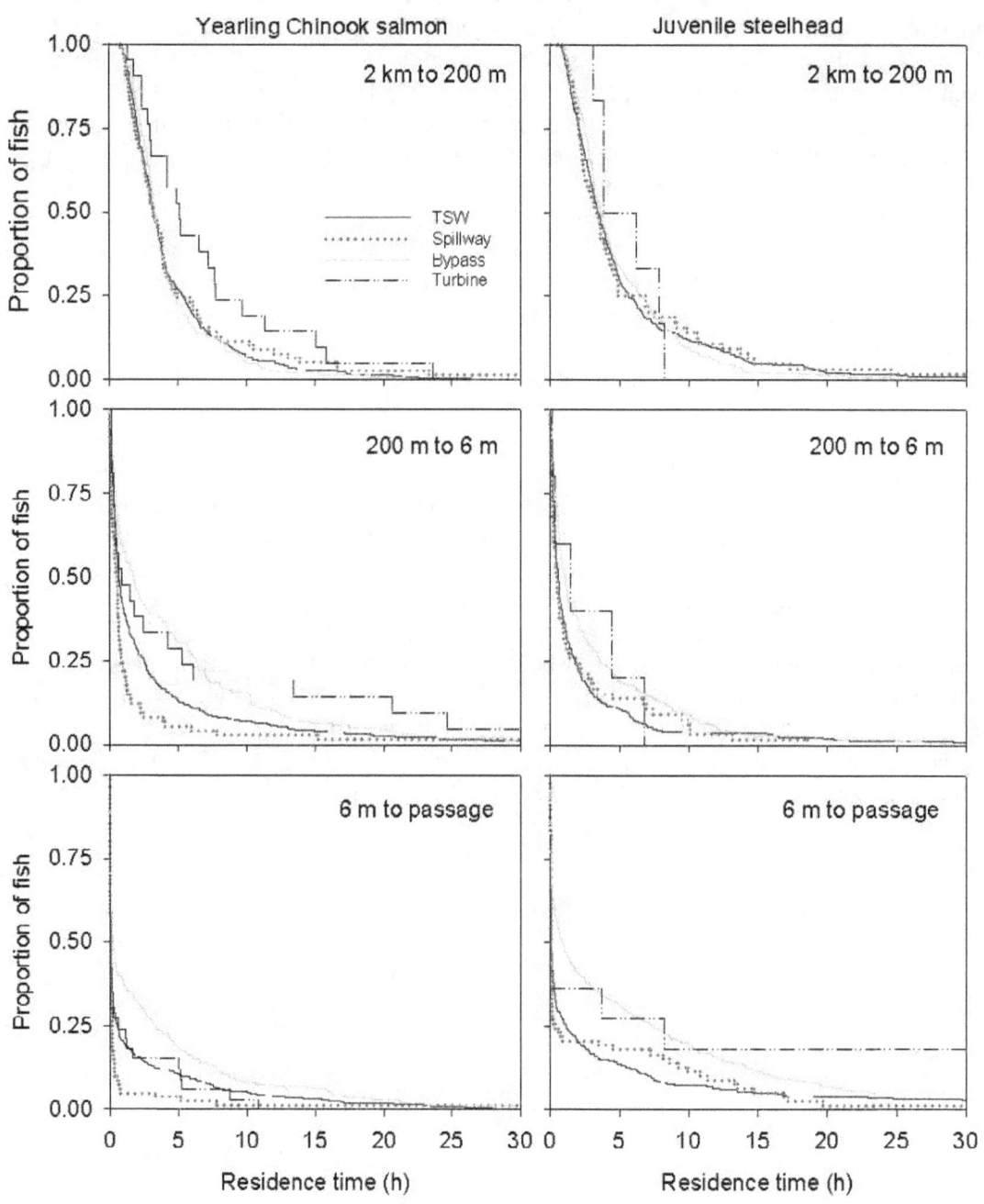

Figure 19. Graphs showing Kaplan-Meier survivorship function (proportion of fish remaining in forebay) of forebay residence time by passage route of yearling Chinook salmon and juvenile steelhead, Little Goose Dam, spring 2009. Few fish passed through the turbines (black line) so plots were truncated after most of the spillway, TSW, and bypass fish passed the dam.

Behavior Near the Trash/Shear Boom

Many yearling Chinook salmon and juvenile steelhead detected in the forebay were detected near the trash/shear boom. Of the 851 yearling Chinook salmon detected in the forebay, 438 (51.5%) were detected near one or more sections of the boom. Similarly, 55.6% (479 of 861) of juvenile steelhead detected in the forebay were detected near the boom. Most fish detected near the boom were first detected at sections within 36 m from the dam. The proportions of first detections near boom sections generally decreased as the distance from the dam increased (table 8).

Table 8. Proportion of first detection of yearling Chinook salmon and juvenile steelhead by distance from the dam along the length of the trash/shear boom, Little Goose Dam, spring 2009.

[N, number of fish; SE represents the standard error of a proportion; m, meter]

Distance	Yearling Chinook salmon			Juvenile steelhead		
	N	Proportion	SE	N	Proportion	SE
12–36 m	188	0.429	0.024	187	0.390	0.022
36–60 m	58	0.133	0.016	64	0.134	0.016
60–84 m	39	0.089	0.014	37	0.077	0.012
84–108 m	26	0.060	0.011	32	0.067	0.011
108–132 m	22	0.050	0.010	50	0.104	0.014
132–156 m	43	0.098	0.014	37	0.077	0.012
156–180 m	19	0.044	0.010	30	0.063	0.011
180–204 m	19	0.043	0.010	18	0.038	0.009
204–228 m	12	0.027	0.008	20	0.042	0.009
228–252 m	12	0.027	0.008	4	0.008	0.004

Movements of yearling Chinook salmon near the boom were in a downstream direction at most sections, but the direction of juvenile steelhead were not. Movements of yearling Chinook salmon were chiefly downstream at sections at least 108 m from the dam, but were about equally upstream and downstream at sections closer to the dam (fig. 20). Net movements of juvenile steelhead were downstream near sections at least 108 m from the dam, in both directions between 60 and 108 m, and in an upstream direction within 60 m of the dam (fig. 20).

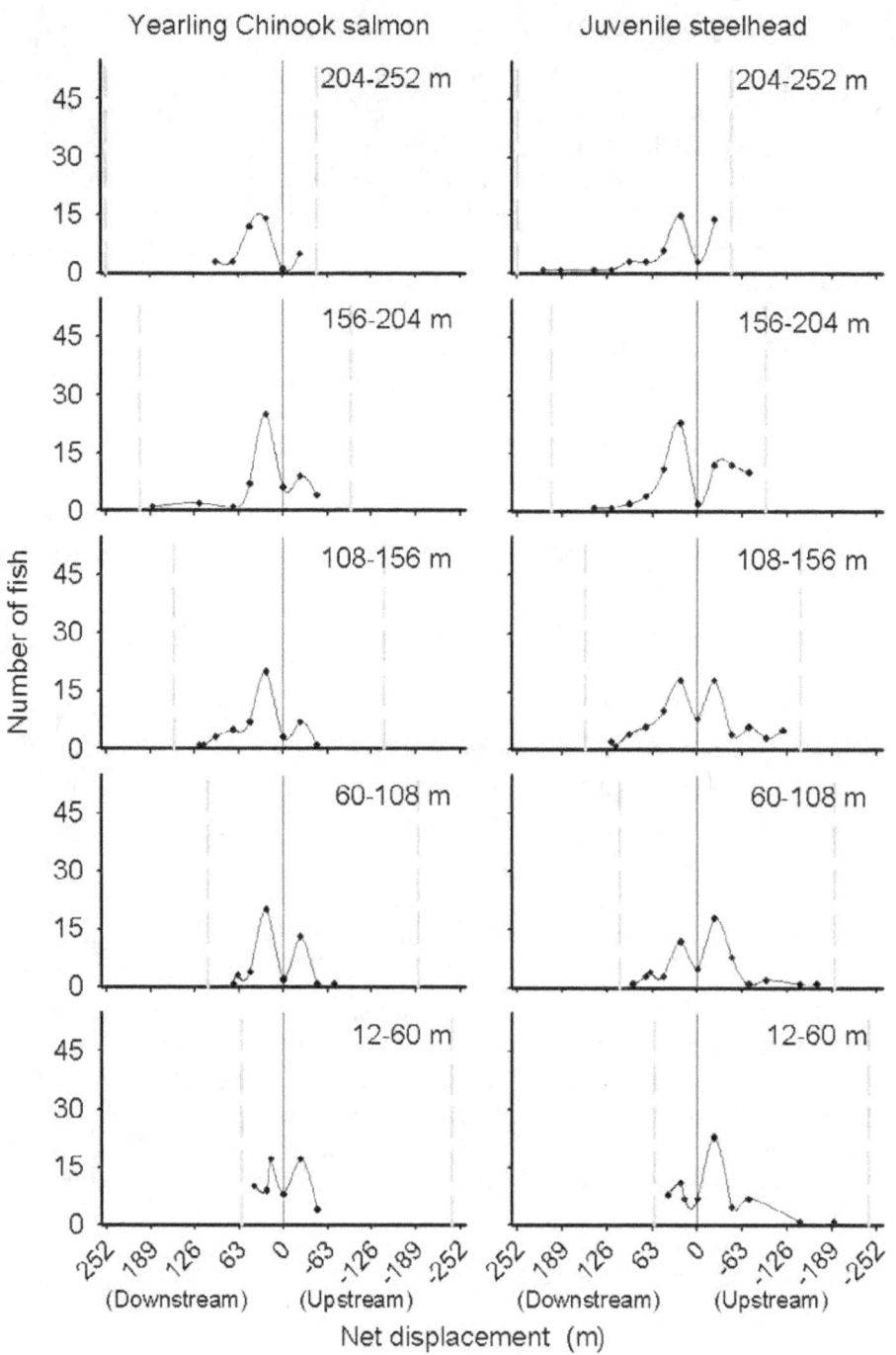

Figure 20. Graphs showing number of radio-tagged yearling Chinook salmon and juvenile steelhead with net displacement by distance from the dam near the trash/shear boom, Little Goose Dam, spring 2009. Distance from the dam is the first contact of the first direct guidance event. Gray vertical dashed lines represent maximum potential net displacement as a result of proximity to the ends of the trash/shear boom.

Route-specific passage proportions of fish detected near the boom differed from proportions of fish never detected near the boom. The powerhouse passage (bypass and turbine) was higher and the spillway and TSW passage were lower for yearling Chinook salmon and juvenile steelhead detected near the boom than for fish not detected near the boom (table 9).

Table 9. Passage proportion by route for yearling Chinook salmon and juvenile steelhead as a function of detection near the trash/shear boom, Little Goose Dam, spring 2009.

[N, number of fish; SE represents the standard error of a proportion]

Species	Passage	Not detected			Detected		
		N	Proportion	SE	N	Proportion	SE
Yearling Chinook salmon	TSW	273	0.667	0.023	252	0.582	0.024
	Spillway	78	0.191	0.019	6	0.014	0.006
	Bypass	47	0.115	0.016	153	0.353	0.023
	Turbine	11	0.027	0.008	22	0.051	0.011
Juvenile steelhead	TSW	199	0.532	0.026	214	0.451	0.023
	Spillway	58	0.155	0.019	21	0.044	0.009
	Bypass	111	0.297	0.024	235	0.494	0.023
	Turbine	6	0.016	0.007	5	0.011	0.005

Rates of Dam Passage

The rate of dam passage varied by route of passage, time spent in the forebay, and the diel period when fish entered the forebay. The rate of passage in this analysis is defined as the proportion of the forebay population passing per hour. Soon after entering the forebay during the day, the passage rate of yearling Chinook salmon was highest through the TSW and lowest through the spillway and bypass; very few fish passed through turbines so that route was omitted from these descriptions. The rate of passage through the TSW generally decreases and the rates of passage through the spillway and bypass remain nearly constant with time spent in the forebay. As such, the proportion of fish that pass through the TSW relative to the other routes decreases and forebay residence time increases. For example, the rate of passage through the TSW is nearly 4 times greater than through the bypass for fish that have been in the forebay for 4 h, but is twice as high as bypass passage for fish that had been in the forebay for 10 h (fig. 21). The trends in passage rates of yearling Chinook salmon entering the forebay during the night were similar to those of fish entering during the day: the greatest rates of passage were through the TSW, followed by the spillway and bypass, and the rate of passage through the TSW decreased with time spent in the forebay. Overall, the rate of yearling Chinook salmon passage was similar for fish that enter the forebay during the day and the night ($\chi^2 = 1.50$, df = 1, $P = 0.2202$). Passage rates of juvenile steelhead entering the forebay during the day were highest through TSW, intermediate for the bypass, and lowest through the spillway. During the night, the order changed and the bypass was the route with the highest passage rate, followed by the TSW and spillway. The rates of juvenile steelhead passage among routes were similar over their range of forebay residence times. Overall, the rate of juvenile steelhead passage was 63% higher for fish that entered the forebay during the night than for fish entering during the day ($\chi^2 = 42.97$, df = 1, $P < 0.0001$).

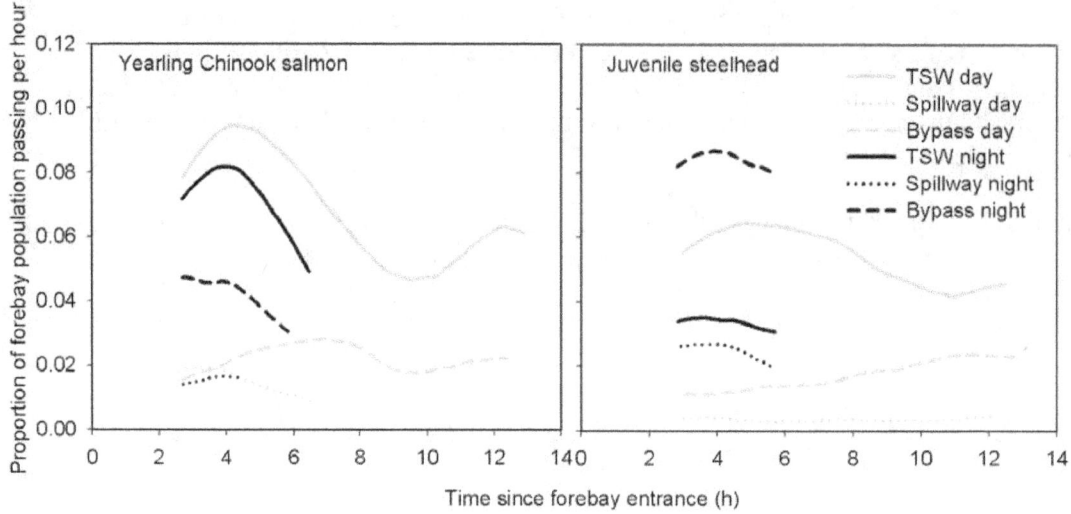

Figure 21. Graphs showing rate of dam passage of yearling Chinook salmon and juvenile steelhead by passage route and diel period at Little Goose Dam, spring 2009. Turbine passage was near zero.

Assessment of Survival Model Assumptions

Negligible bias in survival estimates occurred because of differences in survival rates of fish tagged by the different taggers. Model comparisons supported potential differences in forebay survival probabilities among fish tagged by the four taggers for yearling Chinook salmon and juvenile steelhead (appendix C), but the range among the estimates was small (0.988 to 1.000) and had little effect on the pooled estimates (0.998 and 0.996, respectively). Similarly, the survival estimates of juvenile steelhead control fish from release to the first downstream detection site differed among taggers (range 0.980 to 1.000), but they differed little from the pooled tagger estimate (0.996).

There also was little evidence of bias due to detections of dead fish with live tags. One out of 50 yearling Chinook salmon and 2 out of 50 juvenile steelhead that were euthanized and released at the control site possibly were detected at the second downstream detection array; however, after examining these detections, we believe that these were noise events and not the euthanized fish. Although these events met minimum signal strength criteria and had at least two detections within a 5-min period, the events occurred only at the second downstream array and represented a total of less than or equal to six detections each. None of the 565 yearling Chinook salmon and 585 juvenile steelhead detected at one or more downstream arrays from the control releases were detected only at the second downstream array. Less than 1.3% of the yearling Chinook salmon and less than 2.0% of the juvenile steelhead control fish also had six or fewer detections at the second downstream gate.

Bias because of travel times being longer than the tag life was negligible. The tag-life study indicated that the probability of a radio-tag being operational at downstream detection arrays was greater than 0.997 during spring (appendix B). Thus, most yearling Chinook salmon and juvenile steelhead likely exited the study area prior to expiration of their transmitters.

There was little evidence of a bias in the route-specific survival estimates of yearling Chinook salmon or juvenile steelhead because of differences in post-release mortality of treatment and control groups. Yearling Chinook salmon and juvenile steelhead single-release survival estimates for the reach from the control release site in the tailrace to the first

44

downstream detection array generally were greater or similar to the single-release survival estimates from the point of passage to the first downstream detection array, which was the expected outcome (table D4). In addition, the single-release survival estimates from control fish in the first reach downstream were greater than or equal to 0.98, leaving little room for a bias.

Passage and Survival Probabilities

Survival of yearling Chinook salmon through the pool and forebay was high and few fish passed the dam without a route assignment. Pool and forebay survival probabilities for radio-tagged yearling Chinook salmon were greater than or equal to 0.978 (table 10). We were able to determine a passage location for 99.3% of the fish known to have passed the dam when the low TSW was installed (839 of 845, appendix C). A total of 65.4 % of the fish with known passage routes passed the dam during the day and 34.6 % passed during the night.

Yearling Chinook salmon predominantly passed through the TSW during both the day and the night, followed by the bypass, spillway, and turbines (table 10). However, the probability of passing through the TSW during the day was greater than the probability of passing through the TSW during the night (0.679 versus 0.522). The proportion of fish passing through the bypass increased during the night, concurrent with the decreased passage through the TSW. The probability of fish passing through the bypass was 0.190 during the day and 0.324 during the night. Estimated passage probabilities for spill bays 2–8 and the turbines were low during both the day and the night (≤ 0.107 spillway; ≤ 0.068 turbines). In total, 33 tagged yearling Chinook salmon were detected passing through the turbines (sample sizes are listed in table D1). Differences between day and night passage probabilities were statistically significant for all routes except the spillway (table 10). Overall passage probabilities weighted by the proportion of fish passing during the day and night were TSW, 0.625; bypass, 0.237; spillway, 0.099; and turbines, 0.039 (table 10). The *FGE* and *FPE* were higher during the day than during the night, but the differences were less than 0.065. The overall *FGE* and *FPE* was 0.858 and 0.961 (table 10).

The surface outlet effectiveness for the TSW (*SOS*) was about 12 times greater than the effectiveness for the spillway (*SPS*) during both diel periods (table 10). Both routes were more effective during the day than during the night (day—TSW, 7.077; spillway, 0.572; night—TSW, 5.262; spillway, 0.458), but only the diel difference for the TSW was statistically significant (table 10). The overall *SOS* for the TSW and *SPS* for the spillway was 6.449 and 0.532. The *SPS* for the TSW and spillway combined was 2.779 during the day, 2.129 during the night, and 2.554 overall.

Route-specific estimates of survival of yearling Chinook salmon survival were similar during the day and night. Estimates for the TSW and the bypass were greater than or equal to 0.984 for both diel periods, whereas day and night spillway survival was 0.941 and 0.962, and turbine survival was 0.949 and 0.889 (table 10), respectively. Generally, differences in route-specific survival estimates between day and night were not significant except for the TSW ($P < 0.05$, table 10). Precision was low for the spillway and turbines because few fish passed through these routes. Concrete survival was 0.985 during the day, 1.010 during the night, and 0.994 overall (table 10). The standard errors of the overall concrete survival estimates met the goal of less than or equal to 0.015.

Table 10. Passage probabilities, passage effectiveness, and survival probabilities of yearling Chinook salmon at Little Goose Dam overall and by diel period, spring 2009.

[Estimates, standard errors (SE), and 95% profile likelihood confidence intervals (95% PCI) are presented. Parameter definitions are shown in table 4. Asterisks (*) indicate the 95% PCI for the estimated difference between day and night probabilities does not include zero ($\alpha = 0.05$). Overall estimates were derived from day and night estimates weighted by the proportion of fish passage during each period. Estimates are based on detections of 535 fish passing through the TSW, 84 through spill bays 2–8, 197 through the juvenile bypass, 33 through the turbines, and 27 with an unknown passage route]

	Parameters	Overall Estimate(SE)	Overall 95% PCI	Day Estimate(SE)	Day 95% PCI	Night Estimate(SE)	Night 95% PCI	Day-Night Difference Estimate(SE)	Day-Night Difference 95% PCI
Passage Probabilities	Overall Passage	n/a	n/a	0.654 (0.016)	0.622, 0.685	0.346 (0.016)	0.316, 0.379	0.307 (0.032)	0.243, 0.370*
	Spill bays 2–8	0.099 (0.010)	0.080, 0.121	0.107 (0.013)	0.083, 0.134	0.085 (0.016)	0.057, 0.121	0.022 (0.021)	-0.021, 0.062
	TSW	0.625 (0.017)	0.592, 0.657	0.679 (0.020)	0.640, 0.718	0.522 (0.029)	0.465, 0.579	0.157 (0.035)	0.088, 0.226*
	Bays 2–8 and TSW	0.724 (0.015)	0.694, 0.754	0.786 (0.017)	0.751, 0.819	0.607 (0.029)	0.551, 0.662	0.179 (0.033)	0.114, 0.245*
	Bypass	0.237 (0.015)	0.209, 0.266	0.190 (0.017)	0.159, 0.224	0.324 (0.027)	0.273, 0.379	0.134 (0.032)	0.072, 0.198*
	Turbine	0.039 (0.007)	0.027, 0.054	0.024 (0.006)	0.013, 0.038	0.068 (0.015)	0.043, 0.101	0.045 (0.016)	0.016, 0.079*
	Powerhouse	0.276 (0.015)	0.246, 0.306	0.214 (0.017)	0.181, 0.249	0.393 (0.029)	0.338, 0.449	0.179 (0.033)	0.114, 0.245*
	FGE	0.858 (0.022)	0.809, 0.899	0.890 (0.029)	0.825, 0.938	0.826 (0.035)	0.750, 0.888	0.064 (0.046)	-0.026, 0.155
	FPE	0.961 (0.007)	0.946, 0.970	0.976 (0.006)	0.961, 0.983	0.932 (0.015)	0.899, 0.946	0.045 (0.016)	0.016, 0.079*
Effectiveness	Bays 2–8 (*SPS*)	0.532 (0.055)	0.431, 0.647	0.572 (0.070)	0.444, 0.719	0.458 (0.088)	0.306, 0.648	0.114 (0.112)	-0.115, 0.327
	TSW (*SOS*)	6.449 (0.172)	6.370, 6.600	7.077 (0.207)	6.671, 7.431	5.262 (0.294)	4.690, 5.636	1.815 (0.360)	1.271, 2.451*
	All spill (*SPS*)	2.554 (0.054)	2.445, 2.658	2.779 (0.062)	2.654, 2.896	2.129 (0.100)	1.969, 2.322	0.651 (0.117)	0.422, 0.882*
Survival Probabilities	Pool	0.978 (0.005)	0.967, 0.986	0.977 (0.006)	0.963, 0.987	0.980 (0.008)	0.960, 0.992	0.003 (0.010)	-0.020, 0.022
	Forebay	0.998 (0.002)	0.993, 1.000	0.998 (0.002)	0.992, 1.003	0.997 (0.004)	0.985, 1.000	0.002 (0.004)	-0.006, 0.014
	Spill bays 2–8	0.948 (0.032)	0.873, 1.000	0.941 (0.038)	0.849, 1.001	0.962 (0.058)	0.807, 1.041	0.021 (0.070)	-0.146, 0.147
	TSW	1.001 (0.011)	0.979, 1.023	0.984 (0.014)	0.955, 1.014	1.032 (0.016)	0.997, 1.067	0.048 (0.022)	0.004, 0.092*
	Bays 2–8 and TSW	0.993 (0.011)	0.973, 1.016	0.978 (0.014)	0.950, 1.008	1.022 (0.017)	0.986, 1.058	0.044 (0.022)	-0.001, 0.089
	Bypass	1.016 (0.012)	0.988, 1.040	1.018 (0.014)	0.982, 1.047	1.013 (0.023)	0.957, 1.055	0.005 (0.027)	-0.048, 0.066
	Turbine	0.928 (0.058)	0.770, 1.005	0.949 (0.077)	0.722, 1.031	0.889 (0.084)	0.685, 1.009	0.060 (0.114)	-0.202, 0.292
	Powerhouse	1.004 (0.014)	0.973, 1.030	1.011 (0.016)	0.972, 1.041	0.991 (0.025)	0.934, 1.037	0.020 (0.030)	-0.039, 0.083
	Dam	0.992 (0.010)	0.971, 1.013	0.983 (0.013)	0.958, 1.012	1.007 (0.017)	0.972, 1.043	0.024 (0.022)	-0.020, 0.067
	Concrete	0.994 (0.010)	0.974, 1.015	0.985 (0.013)	0.960, 1.013	1.010 (0.017)	0.976, 1.046	0.025 (0.021)	-0.018, 0.068

46

Estimates of pool and forebay survival of juvenile steelhead were high and few fish passed the dam undetected. Juvenile steelhead survival estimates for the pool and the forebay were greater than or equal to 0.986 (table 11). Passage was assigned to 98.8% of the radio-tagged juvenile steelhead known to have passed the dam (845 of 855; appendix C). A total of 56.4% of these fish passed the dam during the day and 44.6% passed during the night.

The predominant passage route of juvenile steelhead differed between day and night. During the day, juvenile steelhead were much more likely to pass through the TSW than the bypass (0.691 versus 0.267), whereas during the night, this trend reversed and fish were more likely to pass through the bypass than through the TSW (0.586 versus 0.227; table 11). To a lesser degree, the probability of passage through the spillway and turbines also increased during the night relative to the day (0.038 versus 0.163 and 0.004 versus 0.024, respectively). All differences in route-specific day and night passage probabilities were statistically significant (table 11, $P < 0.05$). Overall passage probabilities for the four passage routes were TSW, 0.489; bypass, 0.406; spillway, 0.092; and turbines, 0.013 (table 11). Differences in *FGE* and *FPE* between diel periods were negligible ($\leq$0.024) and overall the estimates were 0.969 for *FGE* and 0.987 for *FPE* (table 11).

Juvenile steelhead TSW and spillway effectiveness varied by the diel period. The TSW effectiveness (*SOS*) was about 35 times greater than for spill bays 2–8 during the day (7.199 versus 0.200), but only about 3 times more during the night (*SOS*, 2.296 versus *SPS*, 0.877). Overall, the *SOS* for the TSW and the *SPS* for spill bays 2–8 were 5.060 and 0.495, respectively. The *SPS* estimates for both routes combined (*SPS* bays 1-8) were day, 2.574; night, 1.370; and overall, 2.049 (table 11).

Juvenile steelhead survival probabilities were high for all passage routes during the day and the night ($\geq$0.984, table 11). Differences between day and night estimates were all less than or equal to 0.039 and were only statistically significant for the turbine route. However, the turbine estimates were based on very few fish (a total of 11 tagged juvenile steelhead; sample sizes are listed in appendix C). The concrete survival estimates were 0.994 for day, 1.002 for night, and 0.998 overall.

Table 11. Passage probabilities, passage effectiveness, and survival probabilities of juvenile steelhead at Little Goose Dam overall and by diel period, spring 2009.

[Estimates, standard errors (SE), and 95% profile likelihood confidence intervals (95% PCI) are presented. Parameter definitions are shown in table 4. Asterisks (*) indicate the 95% PCI for the estimated difference between day and night probabilities does not include zero ($\alpha = 0.05$). Overall estimates were derived from day and night estimates weighted by the proportion of fish passing during each period. Estimates are based on detections of 413 fish passing through the TSW, 79 through spill bays 2–8, 197 through the juvenile bypass, 9 through the turbines, and 25 with an unknown passage route]

	Parameters	Overall		Diel period Day		Night		Day-Night Difference	
		Estimate(SE)	95% PCI	Estimate(SE)	95% PCI	Estimate(SE)	95% PCI	Estimate(SE)	95% PCI
Passage Probabilities	Overall Passage	n/a	n/a	0.564 (0.017)	0.531, 0.596	0.436 (0.017)	0.404, 0.469	0.127 (0.034)	0.061, 0.193*
	Spill bays 2–8	0.092 (0.010)	0.074, 0.113	0.038 (0.009)	0.023, 0.057	0.163 (0.019)	0.128, 0.203	0.126 (0.021)	0.086, 0.168*
	TSW	0.489 (0.017)	0.455, 0.522	0.691 (0.021)	0.649, 0.732	0.227 (0.022)	0.187, 0.272	0.464 (0.030)	0.403, 0.522*
	Bays 2–8 and TSW	0.581 (0.017)	0.548, 0.614	0.728 (0.020)	0.687, 0.767	0.390 (0.025)	0.342, 0.440	0.338 (0.032)	0.274, 0.401*
	Bypass	0.406 (0.017)	0.374, 0.439	0.267 (0.020)	0.229, 0.308	0.586 (0.025)	0.535, 0.635	0.318 (0.033)	0.253, 0.381*
	Turbine	0.013 (0.004)	0.007, 0.022	0.004 (0.003)	-0.017, 0.013	0.024 (0.008)	0.015, 0.043	0.020 (0.008)	0.005, 0.039*
	Powerhouse	0.419 (0.017)	0.386, 0.452	0.272 (0.020)	0.233, 0.313	0.610 (0.025)	0.560, 0.658	0.338 (0.032)	0.274, 0.401*
	FGE	0.969 (0.009)	0.948, 0.976	0.985 (0.011)	0.954, 0.998	0.961 (0.013)	0.930, 0.981	0.024 (0.017)	-0.013, 0.059
	FPE	0.987 (0.004)	0.978, 0.989	0.996 (0.003)	0.987, 0.999	0.976 (0.008)	0.957, 0.983	0.020 (0.008)	0.005, 0.039*
Effectiveness	Bays 2–8 (SPS)	0.495 (0.053)	0.398, 0.606	0.200 (0.046)	0.122, 0.304	0.877 (0.103)	0.688, 1.090	0.677 (0.113)	0.464, 0.906*
	TSW (SOS)	5.060 (0.177)	4.720, 5.365	7.199 (0.221)	6.796, 7.611	2.296 (0.219)	1.897, 2.518	4.903 (0.311)	4.692, 5.299*
	All spill (SPS)	2.049 (0.060)	1.932, 2.165	2.574 (0.072)	2.428, 2.711	1.370 (0.089)	1.199, 1.546	1.204 (0.114)	0.977, 1.425*
Survival Probabilities	Pool	0.986 (0.004)	0.977, 0.993	0.986 (0.005)	0.973, 0.994	0.987 (0.006)	0.972, 0.995	0.001 (0.008)	-0.016, 0.017
	Forebay	0.990 (0.002)	0.990, 0.999	0.996 (0.003)	0.987, 0.999	0.997 (0.003)	0.988, 1.000	0.001 (0.004)	-0.009, 0.011
	Spill bays 2–8	0.997 (0.008)	0.973, 1.008	1.000 (0.000)	1.000, 1.000	0.994 (0.017)	0.939, 1.019	0.006 (0.017)	-0.019, 0.061
	TSW	0.998 (0.006)	0.980, 1.008	0.997 (0.003)	0.987, 1.000	0.999 (0.013)	0.958, 1.021	0.001 (0.014)	-0.039, 0.025
	Bays 2–8 and TSW	0.997 (0.005)	0.984, 1.007	0.997 (0.003)	0.987, 1.000	0.997 (0.011)	0.967, 1.018	0.001 (0.012)	-0.021, 0.030
	Bypass	0.994 (0.007)	0.975, 1.005	0.984 (0.011)	0.952, 0.998	1.006 (0.008)	0.988, 1.024	0.021 (0.013)	-0.002, 0.056
	Turbine	1.005 (0.003)	1.001, 1.012	1.000 (0.000)	1.000, 1.000	1.010 (0.006)	1.002, 1.028	0.010 (0.006)	0.002, 0.027*
	Powerhouse	0.994 (0.007)	0.975, 1.005	0.984 (0.011)	0.953, 0.998	1.006 (0.008)	0.989, 1.024	0.021 (0.013)	-0.002, 0.056
	Dam	0.994 (0.004)	0.984, 1.003	0.990 (0.005)	0.978, 0.996	0.999 (0.008)	0.983, 1.018	0.010 (0.009)	-0.009, 0.031
	Concrete	0.998 (0.004)	0.989, 1.006	0.994 (0.004)	0.984, 0.999	1.002 (0.008)	0.987, 1.021	0.008 (0.008)	-0.008, 0.028

TSW Discovery and Entrance Efficiency

Discovery and entrance efficiencies of yearling Chinook salmon and juvenile steelhead varied by diel period. During the day, 69% of yearling Chinook salmon and 53% of juvenile steelhead detected in the forebay also were detected within 6 m of the TSW (table 12). During the night, the percentages were 52 and 43% for yearling Chinook salmon and juvenile steelhead, respectively. Entrance efficiency, the percentage of fish within 6 m of the route that entered it, was highest for yearling Chinook salmon during the day and for steelhead during the night. More than 94% of fish that came within 6 m of the TSW passed there.

Table 12. Discovery and entrance efficiency (± standard error of a proportion) of yearling Chinook salmon and juvenile steelhead at the Temporary Spillway Weir (TSW) by diel period, Little Goose Dam, spring 2009.

[Discovery efficiency is the number of fish detected within 6 m of the TSW out of all fish detected in the forebay. Entrance efficiency is the number of fish that passed through the TSW out of the number of fish detected within 6 m]

		Discovery efficiency		Entrance efficiency	
Species	Diel period	Numerator/ denominator	Metric	Numerator/ denominator	Metric
Yearling Chinook salmon	Day	354/ 548	0.646 ± 0.020	349/ 354	0.986 ± 0.006
	Night	180/ 303	0.594 ± 0.028	176/ 180	0.978 ± 0.011
	Overall	534/ 851	0.627 ± 0.017	525/ 534	0.983 ± 0.006
Juvenile steelhead	Day	346/ 657	0.527 ± 0.019	329/ 346	0.951 ± 0.012
	Night	87/ 204	0.426 ± 0.035	84/ 87	0.966 ± 0.020
	Overall	433/ 861	0.503 ± 0.017	413/ 433	0.954 ± 0.010

Tailrace Egress

Median egress times varied by species and passage route. Overall median egress times from passage to first detection at the exit site 1.4 km downstream were 15.3 min for yearling Chinook salmon and 14.1 min for juvenile steelhead (table 13). Median egress times of fish passing through the TSW were the shortest and those passing through the turbines were the longest. Median egress times of fish passing through the TSW were 14.9 min for yearling Chinook salmon and 13.4 min for juvenile steelhead (table 13).

Entrainment of fish in the north-shore eddy resulted in an increase in overall tailrace egress times. Only fish that passed through the TSW or spillway were detected in the north-shore eddy. Of the yearling Chinook salmon passing through the TSW, 5.1 % (N =27) were detected in the north shore eddy and 12.5–66.7 % of fish passing through spill bays 2–8 were detected there (23 of 79 for spill bays 2–8). For juvenile steelhead, 5.1% (N = 21) were detected in the eddy after TSW passage and 0–50.0% (22 of 76 for spill bays 2–8) were detected in the eddy after passing through spill bays 2–8. These percentages reflect the magnitude of entrainment in the eddy and include all fish detected there, whereas the tailrace egress times only include fish detected at the tailrace exit site. Median egress times of yearling Chinook salmon detected in the eddy were 12–14 times longer (depending on passage route) than fish not detected in the eddy (fig. 22). The 90th percentile of passage for individual routes was less than 35.1 min for yearling Chinook salmon not entrained in the

49

eddy, but it was more than 405.9 min for those entrained there (fig. 22). Median egress times of juvenile steelhead detected in the eddy also were longer than median egress times of fish not detected there (fig. 22). Median egress time of juvenile steelhead not detected in the eddy after passing through the spillway or TSW was less than 14 min whereas the median egress time of juvenile steelhead detected in the eddy was between 62.4 and 72.8 min after spillway and TSW passage, respectively (fig. 22). The 90th percentile of exiting the tailrace was 53.0 min for steelhead passing through the TSW and not entrained in the eddy, but more than 120.7 min for the remainder of the fish (fig. 22).

Table 13. Descriptive statistics of tailrace egress time of radio-tagged yearling Chinook salmon and juvenile steelhead overall and by passage route at Little Goose Dam, spring 2009.

[Egress time was measured from time of passage to the first detection at the tailrace exit site (1.4 km downstream of dam). Overall egress times are for fish passing through known passage routes. N, number of fish; SE, standard error]

Species	Passage route	N	Mean (SE)	Median (95th CI)	Min.	90%	Max.
Yearling Chinook salmon	TSW	477	48.44 (5.05)	14.93 (13.78–15.80)	3.12	93.22	1,118.63
	Spillway	69	85.25 (20.67)	16.30 (14.13–24.70)	5.53	203.87	1,026.98
	Turbine	27	100.63 (44.83)	22.92 (15.67–37.08)	8.22	229.77	1,162.68
	Overall	573	55.33 (5.34)	15.30 (14.37–16.27)	3.12	111.93	1,162.68
Juvenile steelhead	TSW	383	29.30 (2.38)	13.42 (12.48–14.30)	3.20	66.87	431.65
	Spillway	69	53.36 (8.15)	18.62 (15.18–35.25)	4.22	168.72	304.62
	Turbine	11	366.98 (216.65)	53.30 (35.72–216.28)	22.77	216.28	2,372.43
	Overall	463	41.06 (5.94)	14.13 (13.42–15.05)	3.20	87.82	2,372.43

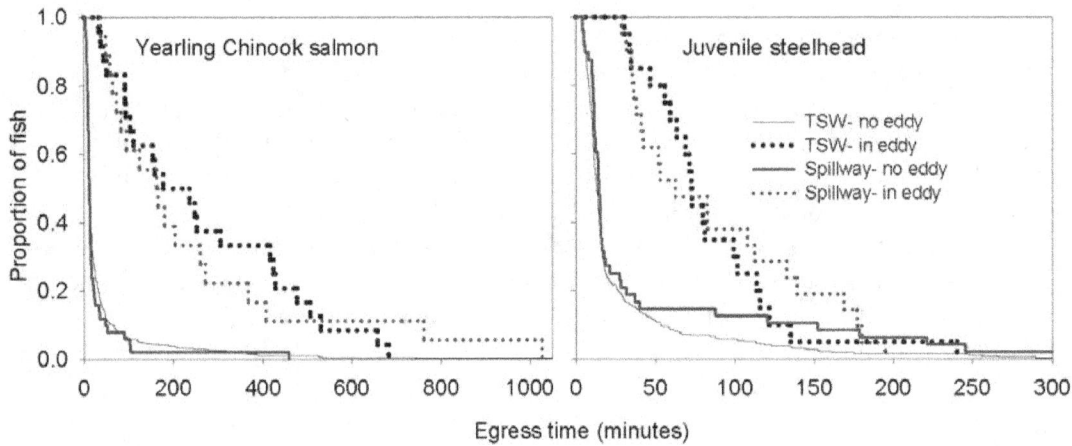

Figure 22. Graphs showing proportion of yearling Chinook salmon and juvenile steelhead remaining in the tailrace (1.4 km reach) after TSW and spill passage by detection in the north shore tailrace eddy at Little Goose Dam, spring 2009. Blue lines depict passage through spill bays 2–8 and black lines depict passage through the TSW. Note the differing x-axis scales.

Summary Migration Period

Dam Operations and Environmental Conditions

Operations during the summer study period consisted of 30% spill and use of the TSW at the low crest elevation during ambient conditions. The summer study period included fish released and detected between June 6 and July 6, 2009. The mean daily discharge during this period ranked third highest in the past 10 years; only 1999 and 2008 were greater (fig. 23). The mean daily project discharge was 93.6 thousand ft^3/s, but ranged from 43.7 to 164.8 thousand ft^3/s during the study period. Daily discharge through the TSW was consistent around the mean of 11.2 thousand ft^3/s, ranging from to 10.6 to 11.6 thousand ft^3/s (fig. 24, appendix D). There was little variation in the percentage of discharge for powerhouse, spillway, and TSW during the day or night. The mean percentage of discharge for powerhouse, spillway, and TSW during the day was 70.6, 17.7, and 11.7%, respectively (29.4% total spillway), compared to 70.4, 17.9, and 11.7% for the powerhouse, spillway, and TSW during the night (29.6% total spillway; fig. 25).

During the 2009 summer study period, there was little difference in daily mean forebay elevation, water temperature, or total dissolved gas compared to the previous 10 years (appendix D). In 2009, the mean daily forebay elevation was consistent at 193.1 m (633.4 ft; NGVD 29), and ranged less than one-half of a meter during the season. The mean daily water temperature was 13.2 °C at the beginning of the study and steadily increased to 19.3 °C by the end of the study. The mean daily total dissolved gas was 109.4% and ranged from 105.0 to 115.7% during the study period (appendix D).

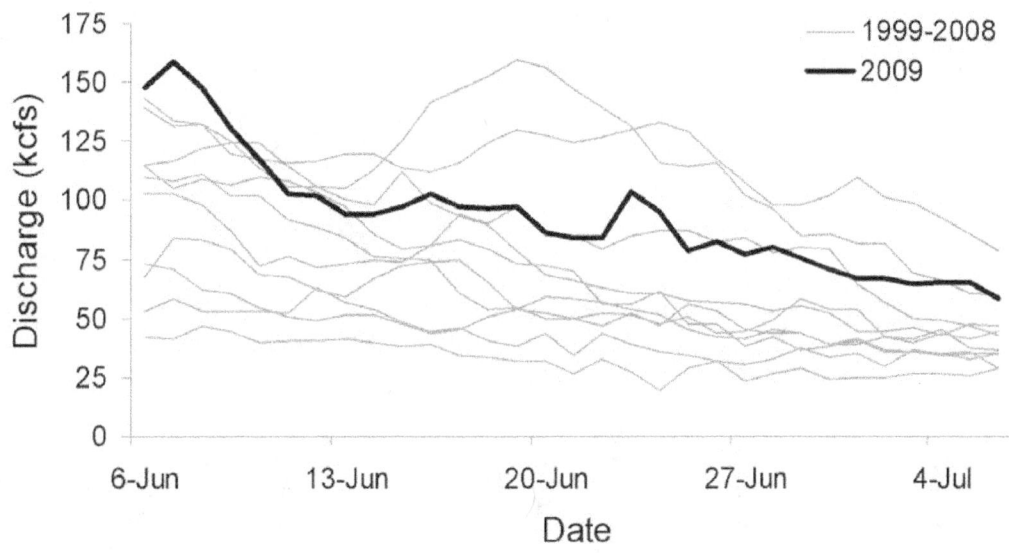

Figure 23. Hydrograph showing total daily project discharge at Little Goose Dam during the summer study period (June 6 to July 6) for the previous 10 years (1999–2008) and current year (2009).

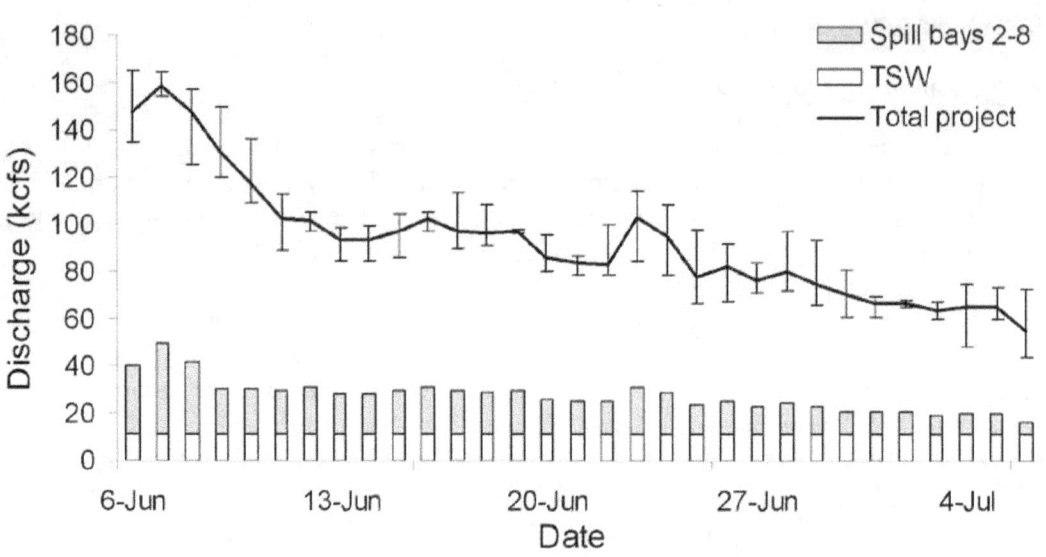

Figure 24. Hydrograph showing mean daily total project discharge (kcfs), TSW discharge (bay 1) and conventional spill discharge (bays 2–8) through Little Goose Dam during the summer study period June 6 to July 6, 2009. Whisker bars represent the minimum and maximum discharge for each day.

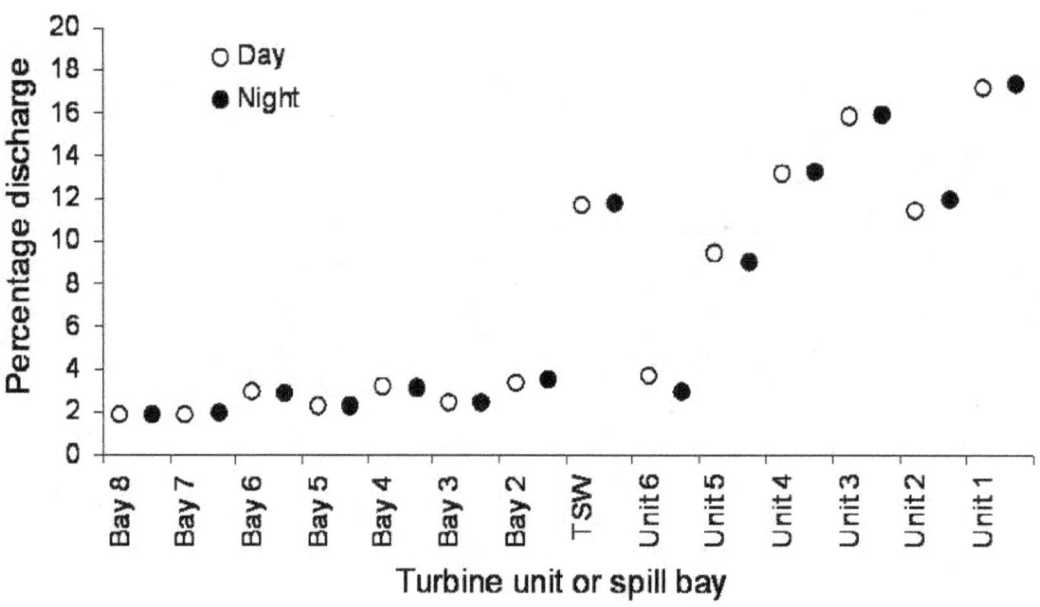

Figure 25. Percentage of total discharge through each turbine unit or spill bay by diel period at Little Goose Dam during the summer study period, June 6 to July 6, 2009.

Tagging and Releasing Fish

The average size of radio-tagged subyearling Chinook salmon differed from the fish sampled at juvenile fish facility with 56% of the fish run meeting our minimum weight criteria of 10 g (fig. 26). Forty-six percent of the run had passed before the study period started on June 6, continuing the trend of earlier run-timing in each of the last 10 years (fig. 27). At the end of the study period, 97% of the subyearling Chinook salmon run had passed Little Goose Dam. Fish sizes of treatment and control groups were similar (table 14). No significant difference was found between the control and treatment group fish weights (t = 0.16, df = 3,533, P = 0.88). Summaries of fish size by release are shown in appendix A.

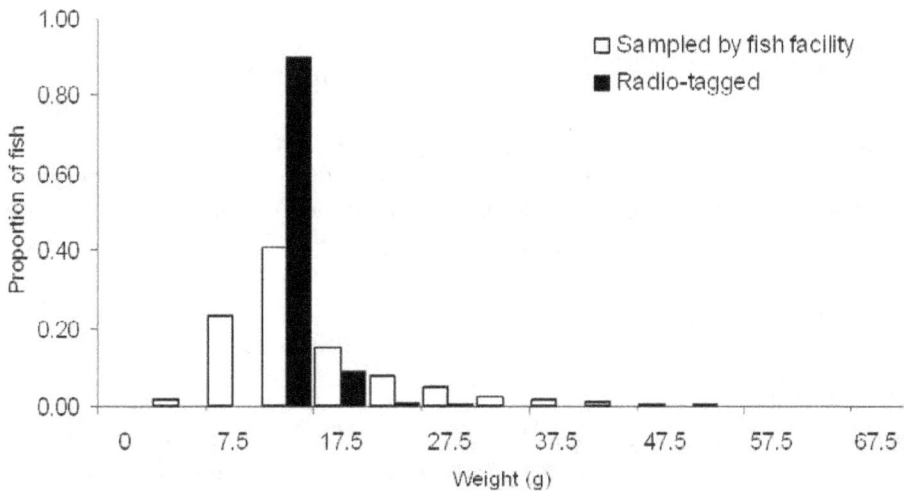

Figure 26. Graph showing frequency distributions of weights for subyearling Chinook salmon collected at the Little Goose juvenile fish bypass facility compared to the frequency distribution of fish radio-tagged during the summer 2009.

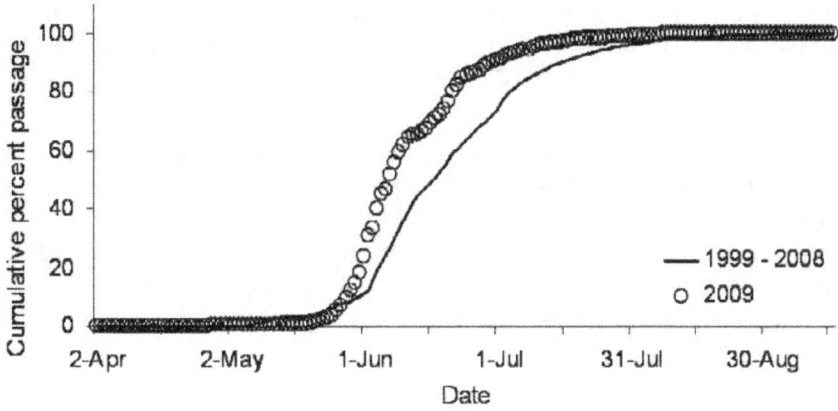

Figure 27. Graph showing cumulative passage distribution of subyearling Chinook salmon at Little Goose Dam. Shown are the historical 10-year average (1999–2008) and the current year (2009). Data from the Fish Passage Center.

53

Table 14. Summary statistics of fork length and weight of radio-tagged subyearling Chinook salmon released at Little Goose Dam, summer 2009.

[N, number of fish; SD, standard deviation]

Release group	N	Fork length, in millimeters			Weight, in grams		
		Mean	SD	Range	Mean	SD	Range
Treatment	2,569	107.1	5.5	96 - 142	12.4	2.3	10.0–32.3
Control	1,632	107.0	5.7	97 - 142	12.3	2.4	10.0–34.5
Euthanized	50	107.7	6.6	100 - 132	12.6	2.9	10.1–25.6

Mortality rates were low during the post-tagging holding period. From June 6 to July 6, 2009, 4,251 (4,201 live and 50 euthanized) subyearling Chinook salmon were radio tagged and released. Post-tagging mortalities were few during the 24-h recovery period for the treatment group (0 of 2,569) and control group 0.11% (2 of 1,680). Tagging mortality rates were within the range of other studies using surgical implantation (Ogden and others, 2005; Perry and others, 2007). In comparison, during the same time period, the mortality rate of subyearling Chinook salmon at the Little Goose Dam juvenile fish facility was 0.94% (data from the Fish Passage Center, www.fpc.org).

Approach Distribution

Subyearling Chinook salmon primarily were detected in the northern portion of the river as they entered the forebay. Subyearling Chinook salmon predominantly were detected first at the north shore antenna (63%) as they passed the telemetry array 2 km upstream of the dam. A total of 24% of tagged subyearling Chinook salmon entered the forebay during the day and 76% entered during the night (fig. 28). Sixty percent of those arriving during the day were detected first at the north shore and 74% of those arriving during the night were detected first at the north shore.

When subyearling Chinook salmon arrived to within 150 m of the dam, they were detected first in greater proportion upstream of the spillway (41%) than the earthen dam (25%) or powerhouse (33%). Difference in area of arrival was small during the day and during the night (fig. 29). This range is slightly shorter than the 200 m range described in the spring migration season because of the different transmitters used in the two study periods and perhaps because of differences in fish behavior. This trend in area of arrival was similar when the new and old earthen dam arrays were used, but the differences among areas were larger when based on the new array.

The first detections of most subyearling Chinook salmon within 6 m of the spillway were near the TSW (fig. 29). This trend was true during the day and night, although during the night, a slightly lower percentage was detected first at the TSW and a slightly larger percentage was detected at spill bay 8.

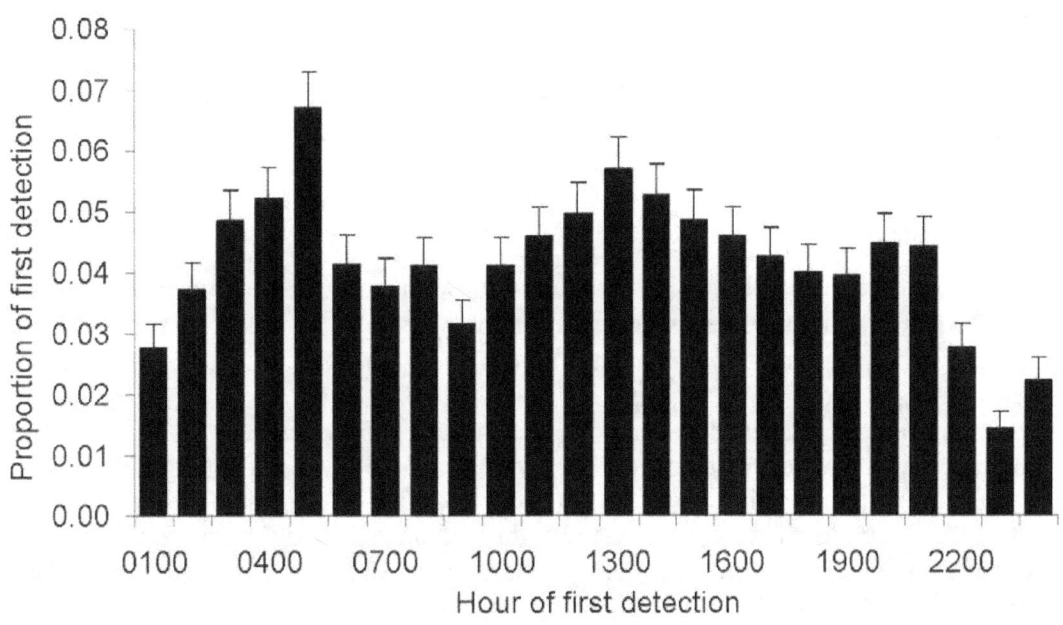

Figure 28. Graph showing proportion of radio-tagged subyearling Chinook salmon (N = 1,878) detected first at the forebay entrance by hour of arrival in 2009. Whisker bars represent the standard error of each hourly proportion.

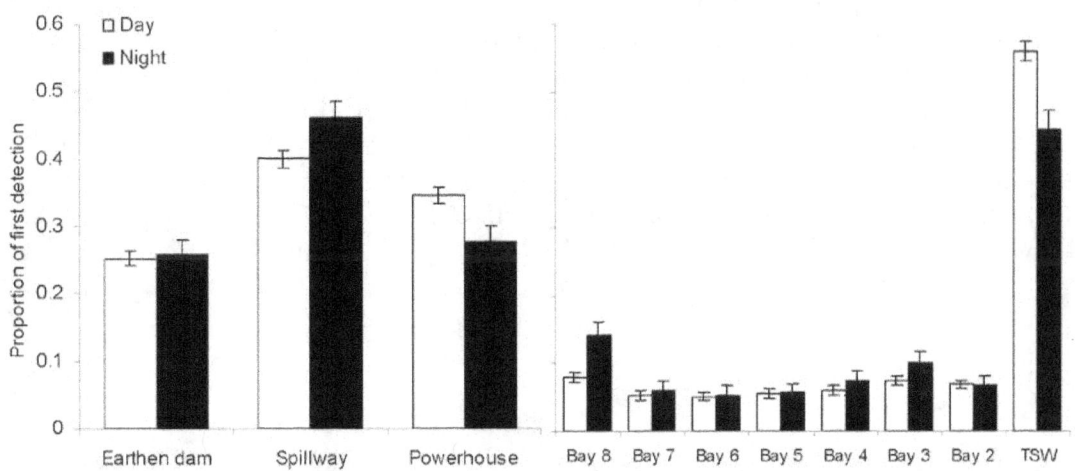

Figure 29. Graph showing proportion of radio-tagged subyearling Chinook salmon detected first within 150 m of the dam (aerial antennas; left plot) and within 6 m of the spillway (underwater antennas; right plot) by diel period in 2009. Whisker bars represent the standard error of each hourly proportion. Sample sizes were 1,523 day and 424 night at the dam and 1,284 day and 297 night at the spillway.

Travel Time

Travel times of subyearling Chinook salmon were similar to those of the spring migrants. Overall, median travel time from release to first detection at the forebay entrance site 2 km upstream of Little Goose Dam was 29.5 h. Travel time ranged from 6.0 to 479.5 h with a mean of 43.5 h.

Forebay Residence Time

Forebay residence times of fish were shorter when entering the forebay during the day than when entering the forebay during the night (χ^2 = 16.28, df = 1, P < 0.0001; fig. 30, appendix E). The median forebay residence times were 5.4 h (95% CI 5.03–5.79 h) for fish entering the forebay during the day and 6.3 h (95% CI 5.09–7.47 h) for fish entering the forebay during the night. The differences between the diel periods were in the latter one-half of the distribution, so the median travel times were similar. However, the 90th percentile of passage (a proportion remaining of 0.10) was 26.7 h for fish entering the forebay during the day and 48.9 h for those entering during the night. Although the maximum forebay residence times were more than 200 h, less than 10% of subyearling Chinook salmon remained in the forebay 48 h after arrival (fig. 30, appendix E). Overall, the median forebay residence time was 5.4 h (95% CI 5.18–5.74 h).

As in the spring, forebay residence times were similar among fish passing through the various routes when the entire 2-km forebay was considered, but differences became evident when fish were closer to the dam. In the reach from 2 km to 150 m upstream of Little Goose Dam, passage route had little influence on the residence time (χ^2 = 15.11, df = 3, P = 0.0017). The median residence time was 2.8 h for TSW, 3.3 h for spill, 3.3 h for bypass, and 2.7 h for turbine fish (fig. 31). In the reach from 150 m to 6 m upstream of the dam, the median residence time for each passage route was similar (range = 0.19 to 1.24 h), but distinct differences were evident later in the distributions. In general, fish passed spillway routes faster than powerhouse routes (χ^2 = 154.41, df = 1, P < 0.0001). Residence times at the 90th percentile were 3.1 h for TSW, 5.7 h for spill, 12.1 h for bypass, and 6.3 h for turbine (fig. 31). More than one-half of fish detected in the final 6-m reach passed within 0.04 h (2.58 min; fig. 31). Residence times for the 90th percentile from 6 m until passage were 2.6 h for TSW, 1.0 h for spill, 12.4 h for bypass, and 8.4 h for turbine fish (fig. 31).

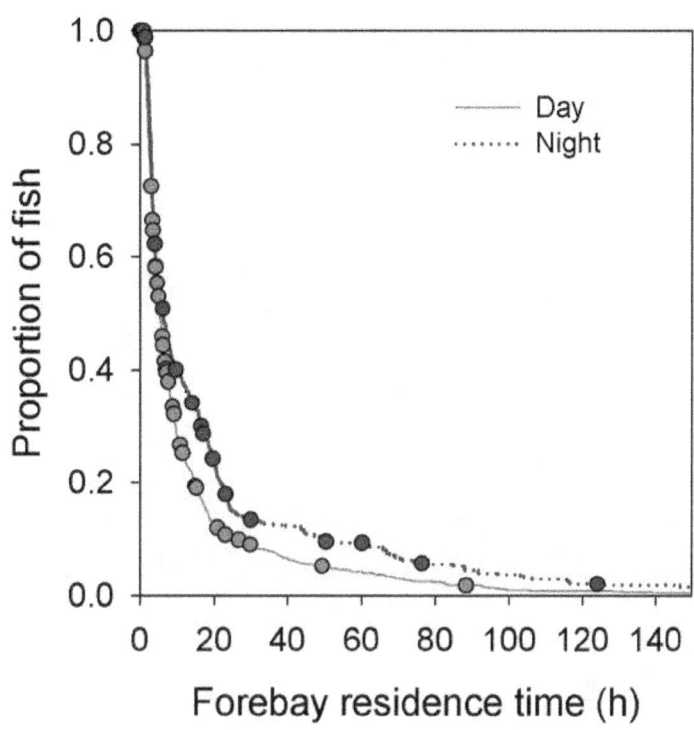

Figure 30. Graph showing Kaplan-Meier survivorship function (proportion of fish remaining in forebay) of forebay residence time by diel period of subyearling Chinook salmon at Little Goose Dam, summer 2009. Circles represent fish detected in the forebay but censored at last forebay detection prior to unknown route of passage.

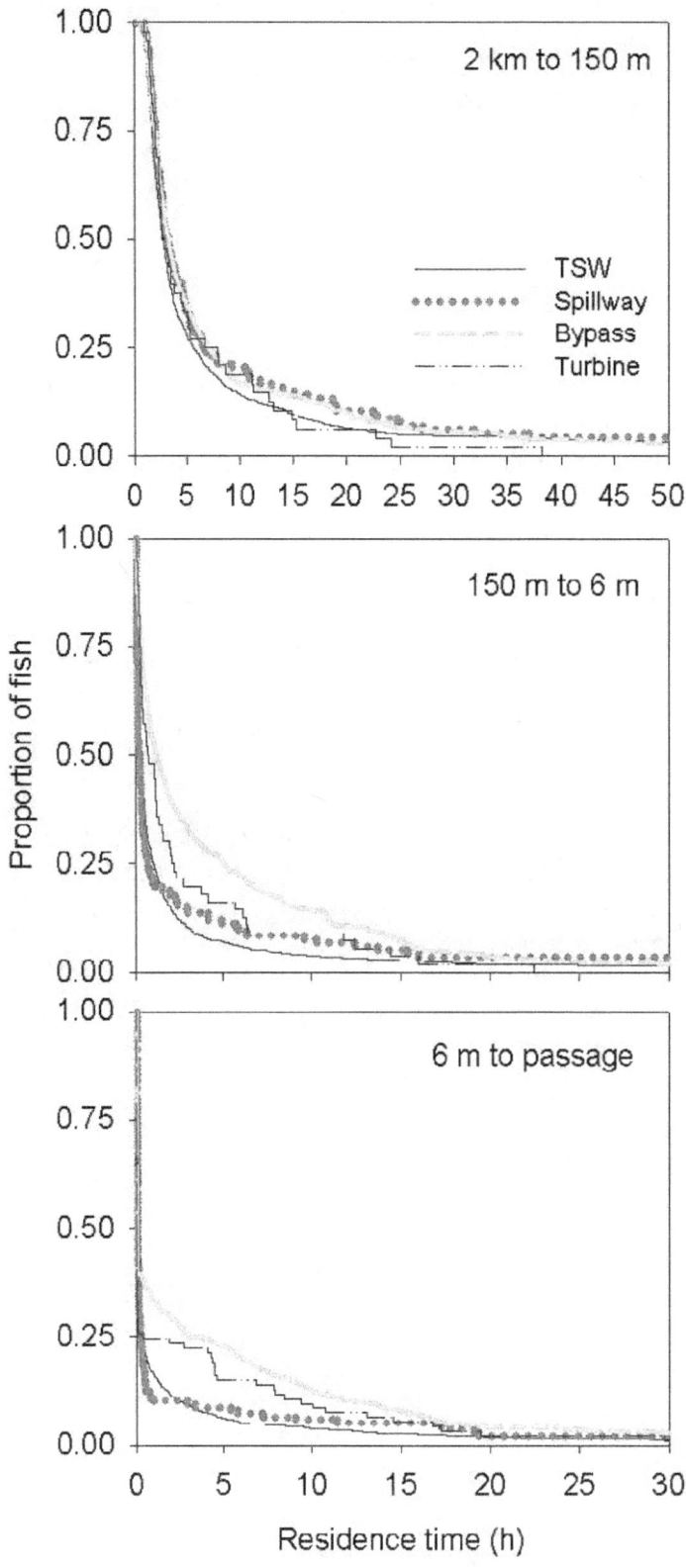

Figure 31. Graphs showing Kaplan-Meier survivorship function (proportion of fish remaining) of forebay residence time by passage route of subyearling Chinook salmon at Little Goose Dam, summer 2009. Note the differing x-axis scales.

Behavior Near the Trash/Shear Boom

Of the 2,280 subyearling Chinook salmon detected in the forebay, 38.9% (888) were detected on one or more sections of the trash/shear boom. Most fish were detected first near the boom at the sections within 36 m of the dam and the proportions of detections decreased with the distance from the dam (table 15). First detections at the boom decreased as distance from the dam increased.

Table 15. Proportion of first detection and standard error (SE) of subyearling Chinook salmon by distance from the dam along the length of the trash/shear boom at Little Goose Dam, summer 2009.

[N, number of fish; SE, standard error]

Distance	N	Proportion	SE
12–36 m	335	0.377	0.016
36–60 m	117	0.132	0.011
60–84 m	88	0.099	0.010
84–108 m	65	0.073	0.009
108–132 m	81	0.091	0.010
132–156 m	73	0.082	0.009
156–180 m	49	0.055	0.008
180–204 m	46	0.052	0.007
204–228 m	16	0.018	0.004
228–252 m	18	0.020	0.005

There was no consistent guidance of subyearling Chinook salmon along the boom. The detections of more than one-half ($N = 561$) of subyearling Chinook salmon detected near the boom indicated either upstream or downstream movement, but there was no overall trend of movement in either direction. The net displacement of fish detected first at the farthest section from the dam were in a downstream direction, but those in all other sections were divided nearly equally between upstream and downstream movement (fig. 32).

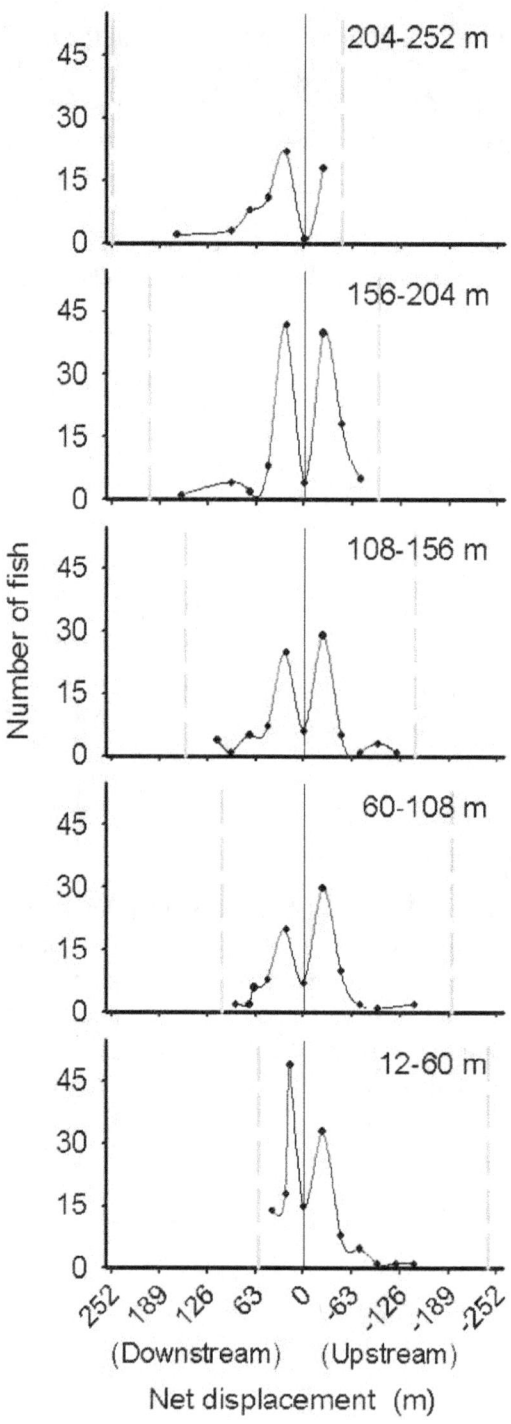

Figure 32. Graph showing number of radio-tagged subyearling Chinook salmon with net displacement by distance from the dam near the trash/shear boom at Little Goose Dam, summer 2009. Distance from the dam is the first contact of the first direct guidance event. Gray vertical dashed lines represent maximum potential net displacement because of proximity to the ends of the trash/shear boom.

60

Spillway and TSW passage was lower and bypass passage was greater for fish detected near the boom than for fish not detected near the boom. Spillway passage was 7% lower, TSW passage was about 10% lower, bypass passage was 16% greater, and turbine passage was similar for fish detected near the boom compared to fish not detected near the boom (table 16).

Table 16. Subyearling Chinook salmon passage proportion and standard error by passage route and detection near the trash/shear boom, Little Goose Dam, 2009.

[N, number of fish; SE, standard error]

Passage	Not detected			Detected		
	N	proportion	SE	N	proportion	SE
TSW	902	0.668	0.013	496	0.574	0.017
Spillway	130	0.096	0.008	19	0.022	0.005
Bypass	266	0.197	0.011	307	0.355	0.016
Turbine	52	0.039	0.005	42	0.049	0.007

Rates of Dam Passage

Passage rates of subyearling Chinook salmon were affected by route of passage, diel period, and length of time in the forebay. Shortly after subyearling Chinook salmon entered the forebay during the day, the passage rate was highest through the TSW and lowest through the spillway and bypass. Fish began passing the dam at the highest overall rate 2–3 h after entering the forebay 2 km upstream of the dam. At this time, the TSW passage rate of fish was 9.8% of the forebay population per hour (that is, hazard = 0.098) whereas bypass and spillway were both less than 1% (fig. 33). The TSW passage rate of fish entering the forebay during the day decreased with increased length of time in the forebay; however, the rate of TSW passage always was greater than spillway and bypass passage. The greatest rate of passage for fish entering the forebay during the night was through the bypass, followed by the TSW and spillway. The relationship between passage rates during the night remained similar regardless of the length of time in the forebay. The rate of turbine passage remained low during the day and night and small sample sizes precluded meaningful plots of the data. Overall, the passage rate during the night was 44% higher than during the day ($\chi^2 = 53.47$, df = 1, $P < 0.0001$).

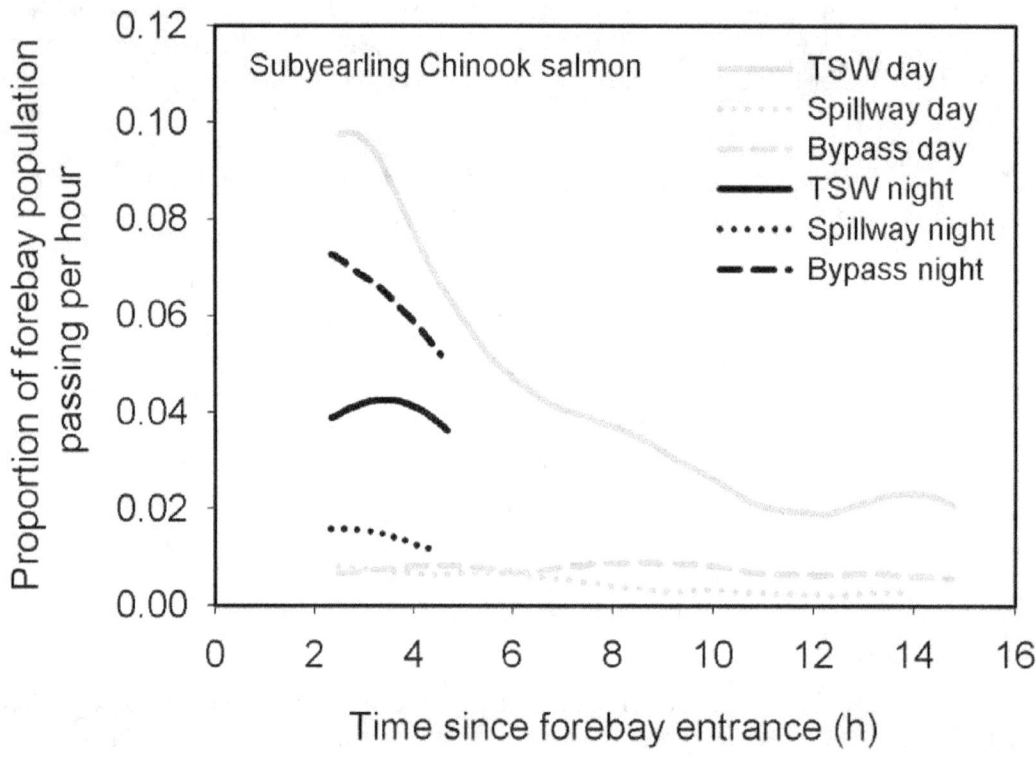

Figure 33. Graph showing rates of passage by passage route and diel period of subyearling Chinook salmon at Little Goose Dam, summer 2009. Turbine passage was near zero.

Assessment of Survival Model Assumptions

The potential for bias in survival probabilities because of detections of dead fish with live tags was negligible. There was one potential detection of a euthanized fish at the first array downstream of the dam and none at the other two downstream arrays. There were 23 detections over a 16-minute interval that met the minimum criteria for a valid detection and careful examination of the records did not reveal anything that would indicate they were noise or otherwise suspect. Four percent of the control fish were detected at only the first downstream array and 45.7% of the control fish detected at this site had 23 or fewer valid detections. Therefore, the first array was excluded from analyses to avoid false-positive detections of dead fish. Possibly one euthanized fish also was detected at the second downstream array, but not at the first or third arrays. However, these detections occurred in two 2-min intervals more than 24 h apart with less than or equal to 13 detections per occasion; these detections are considered to be separate noise events.

Differences in survival estimates based on fish tagged by each of the four taggers were not supported by the data for the pool, forebay, or control releases, but differences in survival between the dam and the first downstream detection array were supported (appendix C). Single-release survival estimates for this reach ranged from 0.802 to 0.867 among taggers. The highest and lowest survival estimates differed significantly between the two taggers (difference = 0.065; 95% PCI: lower bound 0.020, upper bound 0.112), but not the estimates for the other taggers. Because pooled single-release and relative survival estimates were similar with and without the data for the tagger whose fish had the lowest survival (0.837 versus 0.847 and 0.953 versus 0.964), we chose to include the data for all taggers in our estimates.

The probability of tag life being longer than fish travel times was high. We estimated this probability to be greater than 0.987 (appendix C). Thus, the potential for any negative bias in the survival estimates because of non-detection as a result of tag failure was negligible.

There was no evidence of bias in relative survival estimates because of differences in treatment and control survivals downstream of the dam, but the control estimates were low and the potential for bias existed. The single-release survival estimates for the control group downstream of the dam ranged from 0.865 to 0.891, depending on diel period and data pooling, which leaves room for bias to be present. (appendix C). Absence of bias from this source when using the RSSM can be ensured only when the control group survival in the reaches downstream of the dam is 1.000.

Passage and Survival Probabilities

Survival through the pool and forebay was high and few fish passed the dam without a route assignment. Subyearling Chinook salmon pool survival was estimated to be ≥ 0.922 and forebay survival was estimated to be ≥ 0.984 (table 17). For the route-specific survival evaluation, passage was assigned to 98.2% of the radio-tagged fish passing the dam (2,169 of 2,209; appendix C). We estimated that 68.2% of these fish passed the dam during the day and 31.8% passed at night. Subyearling Chinook salmon passing the dam when the TSW crest was changed from low to high were omitted from analysis. Of these 79 subyearling Chinook salmon, 22 passed after the high crest was installed (bypass, 4; TSW, 10; undetermined passage, 8).

The most common route of passage was the TSW. The probability of passage through the TSW (0.646) was nearly 3 times greater than the probability of passage through the bypass (0.244), about 10 times greater than through the spillway (0.068), and 15 times greater than through the turbines (0.042; table 17). As in the spring, the turbine route was the least common; the estimates of turbine passage were based on 94 tagged subyearling Chinook salmon detected passing that route (see appendix C for sample sizes of tagged fish).

Route-specific passage probabilities differed during the day and night. During the day, the probability of passage through the TSW (0.780) was substantially greater than the probability of passing through any other route (bypass 0.157, spillway 0.054, turbine 0.009; table 17). During the night, the probability of passing through the TSW was much less than during the day and the greatest passage probability was at the bypass (bypass, 0.430; TSW, 0.361; spillway, 0.097; turbine, 0.112; table 17). All diel differences in route-specific passage probabilities were statistically significant ($P < 0.05$, table 17). The *FGE* and *FPE* were significantly greater during the day than during the night (0.943 versus 0.793 for *FGE* and 0.991 versus 0.888 for *FPE*) and overall *FGE* was 0.852 and *FPE* was 0.958 (table 17).

The surface outlet effectiveness of the TSW (*SOS*) was about 21 times greater than the effectiveness for spill bays 2–8 (*SPS*) during the day (6.6 versus 0.307), but only about 6 times greater at night (*SOS*, 3.0; *SPS*, 0.54; table 17). Overall, the *SOS* was 5.4 and the SPS for the spillway was 0.383 (table 17). The *SPS* estimates for both routes combined were 2.8 for day, 1.5 for night, and 2.4 for overall.

Route-specific survival probabilities were highest for subyearling Chinook salmon that passed through the TSW during the day and the TSW or bypass at night (≥ 0.974), but otherwise were relatively low for fish passing through the bypass, spillway, and turbine (range: 0.812 to 0.880, table 17). Except for the TSW, survival estimates were lower during the day than during the night (bypass, 0.877 versus 0.976; spillway, 0.839 versus 0.880; turbine, 0.812 versus 0.861; table 17). However, only the diel differences in survival for the bypass were statistically significant, with survival at night being higher than during the day (table 17). The precision of the spillway and the turbine survival estimates was relatively low because fewer tagged fish passed through these routes. The overall survival probabilities for the four passage routes were TSW, 0.975; bypass, 0.908; spillway, 0.852; and turbine, 0.828 (table 17). The concrete survival estimates were 0.950 during the day, 0.954 during the night, and 0.952 for overall (table 17). The standard error of the overall concrete survival estimate met the goal of ≤ 0.015.

64

Table 17. Passage probabilities, passage effectiveness, and survival probabilities of subyearling Chinook salmon at Little Goose Dam overall and by diel period, summer 2009.

[Estimates, standard errors (SE), and 95% profile likelihood confidence intervals (95% PCI) are presented. Parameter definitions are shown in table 4. Asterisks (*) indicate the 95% PCI for the estimated difference between day and night probabilities does not include 0 ($\alpha = 0.05$). Overall estimates were derived from day and night estimates weighted by the proportion of fish passing during each period. Estimates are based on detections of 1,398 fish passing through the TSW, 149 through spill bays 2–8, 528 through the juvenile bypass, 94 through the turbines, and 273 with an unknown passage route]

| | Diel period | | | | | | | |
| | Overall | | Day | | Night | | Day-Night Difference | |
Parameters	Estimate(SE)	95% PCI	Estimate(SE)	95% PCI	Estimate(SE)	95% PCI	Estimate(SE)	95% PCI
Passage Probabilities								
Overall Passage	n/a	n/a	0.682 (0.009)	0.663, 0.700	0.318 (0.009)	0.300, 0.337	0.364 (0.013)	0.327, 0.400*
Spill bays 2–8	0.068 (0.005)	0.058, 0.079	0.054 (0.006)	0.043, 0.066	0.097 (0.011)	0.077, 0.120	0.043 (0.005)	0.019, 0.068*
TSW	0.646 (0.010)	0.627, 0.666	0.780 (0.011)	0.758, 0.800	0.361 (0.018)	0.326, 0.397	0.419 (0.021)	0.377, 0.460*
Bays 2–8 and TSW	0.714 (0.010)	0.695, 0.733	0.834 (0.010)	0.814, 0.852	0.458 (0.019)	0.421, 0.495	0.376 (0.021)	0.334, 0.418*
Bypass	0.244 (0.009)	0.226, 0.262	0.157 (0.009)	0.139, 0.176	0.430 (0.019)	0.393, 0.467	0.273 (0.021)	0.232, 0.315*
Turbine	0.042 (0.004)	0.034, 0.051	0.009 (0.003)	0.007, 0.015	0.112 (0.012)	0.090, 0.137	0.103 (0.012)	0.080, 0.128*
Powerhouse	0.286 (0.010)	0.267, 0.305	0.166 (0.010)	0.148, 0.186	0.542 (0.019)	0.505, 0.579	0.376 (0.021)	0.334, 0.418*
FGE	0.852 (0.014)	0.824, 0.879	0.943 (0.015)	0.909, 0.967	0.793 (0.021)	0.750, 0.831	0.150 (0.025)	0.100, 0.199*
FPE	0.958 (0.004)	0.949, 0.960	0.991 (0.003)	0.985, 1.037	0.888 (0.012)	0.863, 0.909	0.103 (0.012)	0.080, 0.128*
Effectiveness								
Bays 2–8 (*SPS*)	0.383 (0.030)	0.326, 0.445	0.307 (0.033)	0.246, 0.377	0.544 (0.062)	0.431, 0.674	0.237 (0.071)	0.103, 0.381*
TSW (*SOS*)	5.431 (0.085)	5.263, 5.588	6.551 (0.090)	6.370, 6.724	3.032 (0.154)	2.735, 3.335	3.519 (0.179)	3.379, 3.863*
All spill (*SPS*)	2.417 (0.032)	2.352, 2.480	2.826 (0.033)	2.760, 2.888	1.541 (0.064)	1.416, 1.667	1.285 (0.072)	1.144, 1.423*
Survival Probabilities								
Pool	0.922 (0.006)	0.911, 0.933	0.922 (0.007)	0.908, 0.934	0.924 (0.010)	0.903, 0.941	0.002 (0.012)	-0.022, 0.025
Forebay	0.984 (0.003)	0.977, 0.990	0.980 (0.004)	0.971, 0.988	0.992 (0.005)	0.980, 1.001	0.012 (0.007)	-0.002, 0.025
Spill bays 2–8	0.852 (0.044)	0.762, 0.932	0.839 (0.057)	0.720, 0.942	0.880 (0.062)	0.750, 0.991	0.041 (0.084)	-0.125, 0.205
TSW	0.975 (0.015)	0.945, 1.006	0.974 (0.017)	0.941, 1.010	0.977 (0.031)	0.914, 1.036	0.003 (0.035)	-0.069, 0.070
Bays 2–8 and TSW	0.963 (0.015)	0.934, 0.991	0.966 (0.017)	0.933, 1.000	0.957 (0.029)	0.899, 1.012	0.009 (0.033)	-0.056, 0.076
Bypass	0.908 (0.024)	0.859, 0.955	0.877 (0.033)	0.810, 0.940	0.976 (0.029)	0.918, 1.031	0.099 (0.044)	0.013, 0.186*
Turbine	0.828 (0.096)	0.623, 0.980	0.812 (0.138)	0.518, 1.027	0.861 (0.059)	0.739, 0.968	0.049 (0.150)	-0.204, 0.364
Powerhouse	0.898 (0.024)	0.851, 0.944	0.873 (0.032)	0.808, 0.935	0.952 (0.027)	0.898, 1.005	0.079 (0.042)	-0.003, 0.163
Dam	0.936 (0.013)	0.911, 0.963	0.932 (0.017)	0.900, 0.965	0.947 (0.022)	0.904, 0.990	0.015 (0.027)	-0.039, 0.069
Concrete	0.952 (0.013)	0.926, 0.978	0.950 (0.017)	0.919, 0.984	0.954 (0.022)	0.911, 0.998	0.004 (0.013)	-0.050, 0.058

TSW Discovery and Entrance Efficiency

The TSW discovery efficiency varied by diel period, but the TSW entrance efficiency did not. During the day, 67% of fish in the forebay came within 6 m of the TSW compared to only 46% of fish during the night (table 18). More than 98% of the fish that came within 6 m of the TSW passed that route (table 18).

Table 18. Discovery and entrance efficiency (± standard error of a proportion) of subyearling Chinook salmon at the TSW overall and by diel period, Little Goose Dam, summer 2009.

[Discovery efficiency is the number of fish detected within 6 m of the TSW out of all fish detected in the forebay. Entrance efficiency is the number of fish that passed through the TSW out of the number of fish detected within 6 m. Diel period is assigned at first detection in the Little Goose Dam forebay]

| Diel period | Discovery efficiency | | Entrance efficiency | |
	Numerator/ denominator	Metric	Numerator/ denominator	Metric
Day	1,114/ 1,747	0.638 ± 0.012	1,106/ 1,114	0.993 ± 0.003
Night	295/ 536	0.550 ± 0.022	292/ 295	0.990 ± 0.006
Overall	1,409/ 2,283	0.617 ± 0.010	1,398/ 1,409	0.992 ± 0.002

Tailrace Egress

Median egress times of radio-tagged subyearling Chinook salmon varied by passage route. The overall median egress time from passage to first detection at the exit site 1.4 km downstream was 18.2 min (table 19). The median egress times were 17.7 min for fish passing through the TSW, 28.6 min for those passing the turbines, and 38.6 min for those passing the spillway (table 19).

Few subyearling Chinook salmon were detected in the north shore eddy after dam passage. Three percent of fish passing through the TSW, 31% of those passing the other spill bays, and one fish passing the turbines were detected in the north shore eddy. Median egress times of the fish detected in the eddy were more than 5 times longer than those not detected there.

Entrainment in the north shore eddy altered the entire distribution of egress times. Median egress times for fish entrained in the eddy were 92.8 min for spillway passage (95% CI 74.88–151.92 min) and 177.0 min for TSW passage (95% CI 103.18–221.73; fig. 34). In addition to the differences in the median times, the 90th percentile of spillway or TSW passage was less than 125.7 min for fish not entrained in the eddy, but it was more than 245.1 min for those entrained there (fig. 34). Entrainment in the eddy increased egress times of fish that passed the TSW more than for fish passing the other spill bays.

Table 19. Descriptive statistics of tailrace egress time of radio-tagged subyearling Chinook salmon by passage route and overall at Little Goose Dam, summer 2009.

[Egress time was measured from time of passage to the first detection at the tailrace exit site (1.4 km downstream of dam). Overall egress times are for fish passing through known passage routes. N, number of fish; SE, standard error]

Passage route	N	Mean ± SE	Median (95% CI)	Min.	90%	Max.
TSW	1,066	43.12 ± 2.50	17.73 (17.12–18.40)	6.25	81.70	1,016.50
Spillway	117	89.96 ± 13.69	38.65 (21.53–44.50)	6.27	202.52	936.62
Turbine	75	126.24 ± 81.97	28.65 (21.03–31.92)	9.88	78.05	6,173.18
Overall	1,258	52.43 ± 5.49	18.20 (17.57–19.47)	6.25	95.62	6,173.18

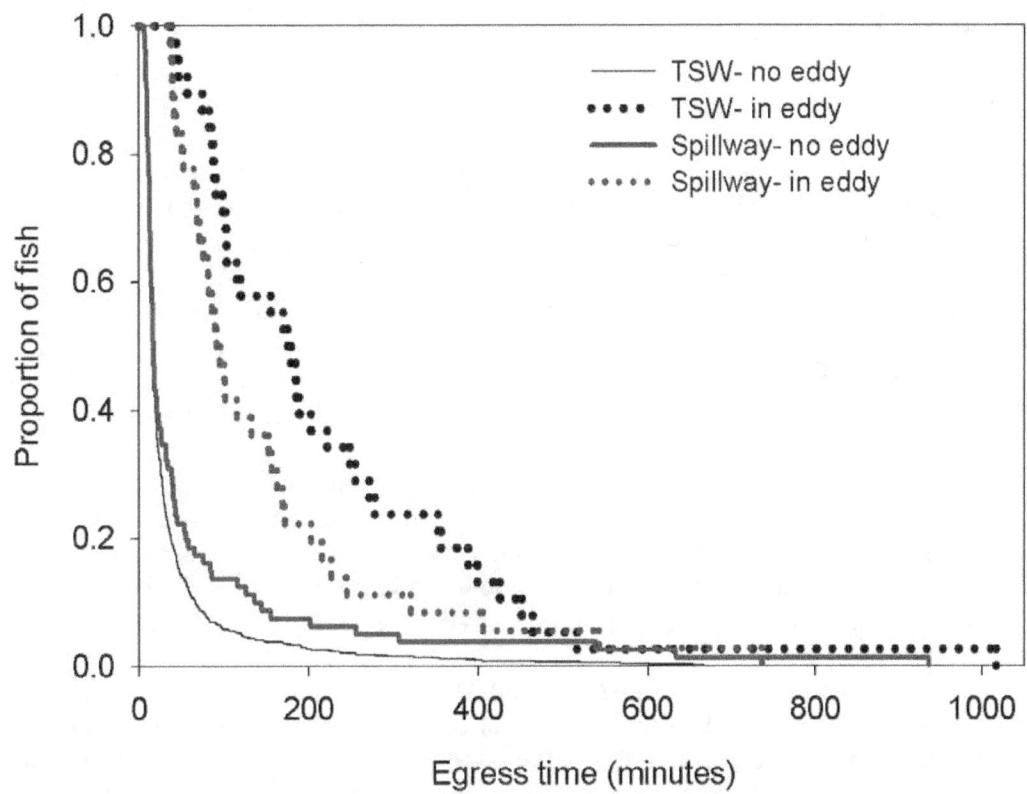

Figure 34. Graph showing proportion of subyearling Chinook salmon remaining in the tailrace (1.4 km reach) after TSW and spill passage by detection in the north shore tailrace eddy at Little Goose Dam, summer 2009. Blue lines depict passage through spill bays 2–8 and black lines depict passage through the TSW.

Discussion

The studies at Little Goose Dam in 2009 mark the first in what will likely be a series of studies to evaluate the performance of the spillway weir implemented in 2009. This study indicates that the operation of dam with the low-crest TSW during 30% 24-h spill resulted in low probabilities of turbine passage, low probabilities of passage through conventional spill bays, high probabilities of TSW passage, and high probabilities of concrete survival. The TSW was the most common route of passage. More than 62% of juvenile Chinook salmon and 49% of juvenile steelhead passed through this route. All groups of fish studied had more powerhouse passage and less TSW and spillway passage during the night than during the day. This trend is common at dams in the Columbia River Basin and has been shown previously at Little Goose Dam (Perry and others, 2007; Beeman and others, 2008a, 2008b). As in previous years, yearling and subyearling Chinook salmon exhibited a diel shift to greater powerhouse passage during the night in 2009 (Beeman and others, 2008a, 2008b). Juvenile steelhead had a diel shift to greater powerhouse passage during the night in 2007 and 2009, but in 2006, powerhouse and spillway passage was similar during the day and night (Beeman and others, 2008a, 2008b). The increased powerhouse passage during the night has not resulted in increased turbine passage of yearling Chinook salmon or juvenile steelhead, because their *FGE* is high and is similar during the day and night. However, the diel shift does result in greater turbine passage of subyearling Chinook salmon during the night, as their *FGE* generally is lower during the night than during the day (Beeman and others, 2008a, 2008b). The increases in turbine passage of subyearling Chinook salmon during the night have not resulted in a decrease in overall dam passage survival in any of the years that have been studied to date (Perry and others, 2007; Beeman and others, 2008a, 2008b).

Data from similar water years are not available to compare with the data from 2009. The nearest water year with data available is 2006 during the spring and summer. The two water years were similar during the spring, but in the summer, the river discharge in 2006 was 71% of the river discharge in 2009. The median discharges between June 6 and July 6, the summer study dates in 2009, were 66.5 thousand ft^3/s in 2006 and 93.9 thousand ft^3/s in 2009. Forebay residence times of yearling Chinook salmon and juvenile steelhead in 2009 were less than 1 h different than forebay residence times in 2006 (the median values in 2009 were less than 8 h), but those of subyearling Chinook salmon were less than one-half of those from 2006 (5.4 versus 12.2 h). We cannot determine if the TSW affected forebay residence times, because it was only present in 2009 and the environmental and operating conditions were different among years.

Dam operation with the TSW in 2009 resulted in a shift in the spillway passage location compared to previous years, but had little effect on survival. At Little Goose Dam, the forebay residence times of spring migrants in years with 30% spill generally are short and survival in the forebay is high (>0.98 in 2009). Forebay survival of subyearling Chinook salmon also generally is high (0.98 in 2009). The net result of operation with the TSW is difficult to estimate because there was no experimental manipulation of the weir in 2009 and differences in water years may affect year-to-year comparisons. However, it is clear that in 2009, the TSW decreased passage through conventional spill bays (bays 2–8) compared to the passage that would have occurred without the TSW. Fish survival through all routes other than the turbines, for which the estimates are imprecise, generally are high and similar to one another. Thus, changes in the locations of non-turbine passage have had little effect on the concrete survival of juvenile salmonids at this dam. This finding may change if the amount of water spilled is reduced, because the effectiveness of the TSW is much greater than conventional spill bays, and the overall probability of spillway passage (TSW plus conventional bays) would be higher with the TSW present than without it.

The 2009 study design included evaluating both "low" and "high" crest TSW configurations, but data were only collected in the "low crest" configuration because of high summer discharge. The intent of the 2-elevation weir at Little Goose Dam is to use the "low-crest" elevation when total river discharge is greater than 75 thousand ft^3/s and change to the "high crest" elevation when discharge is likely to be low for an extended period. The reason for this operation is that the amount of water passing through the weir is controlled by the forebay elevation, not the river discharge, and at low river discharges most, or all, of the 30% of total discharge available for spill might be passed through the TSW. This could leave little or no water to pass through other spill bays for control of tailrace egress conditions ("training spill"). Changing to a higher crest during low river discharge reduces the water passing through the weir and increases the amount of water available for training spill. In 2009, the river discharge was not near this threshold level until the end of the fish release schedule, so the fishery managers agreed to postpone the weir change until this study was completed. The alternative was to change the weir elevation with only a few days remaining in fish releases, which likely would have resulted in too little data from which to make reliable inference during the high crest operation. Empirical data are not available on passage and survival of volitionally passing juvenile salmonids with the TSW at the high crest elevation.

Tagged fish did not appear to be guided toward or away from the dam along the trash/shear boom. Some fish were detected moving upstream and others were detected moving downstream near the boom, which is consistent with results from 2007 (Beeman and others, 2008a). Fish detected near the boom were more likely to pass through the powerhouse than the spillway or TSW, but we cannot infer causation from the data collected in 2009. We hypothesize that many of the fish detected near the boom were fish that did not pass the dam soon after their arrival and were travelling throughout the forebay. If so, these results indicate that the higher powerhouse passage of fish detected near the boom was coincidental rather than causative.

The results of the present study indicate that direct plus indirect survival of fish passing through the TSW are higher than the direct survival described by Normandeau Associates and others (2009). We estimated that the survival of yearling Chinook salmon and juvenile steelhead passing the TSW was near 1.0 and that of subyearling Chinook salmon was 0.975 (SE 0.02). Normandeau Associates and others (2009) estimated the survival of fish passed through the TSW operated at its low crest elevation was 0.97 (SE 0.01) during the first 24 h after passage and 0.95 (SE 0.01) 48 h after passage. The expectation is that the direct plus indirect survival would be lower than the direct survival, yet in 2009, the results were similar. The two studies differ in several ways that may explain this outcome, such as the fish source, time of year, the methods, and the elevation of fish passing the TSW. The latter difference has been shown to affect direct survival, with fish that are released deeper having lower survival (Normandeau Associates and others, 2008). Normandeau Associates and others (2009) released test fish through a pipe 1.5 ft (0.46 m) above the ogee crest of the TSW, whereas the fish in this study passed volitionally. Recent data from Lower Monumental Dam indicates that volitionally passing fish are nearer to the water surface than the ogee crest (Ham and others, 2009), supporting the hypothesis that differences in passage depths between the balloon-tag and radio-tag studies may explain the differences in the results of the two studies.

The regional trend toward active tags (that is, radio or acoustic transmitters) and away from active hydroacoustics to assess fish passage does not allow for an unbiased measure of the diel distribution of juvenile salmonids. These data are not likely to be collected from fish with active tags because of the effect of release time, location, and date. Without data from the untagged population, diel differences in survival of tagged fish can result in biased estimates of dam passage survival. As such, these data should be weighted by the diel passage distribution of untagged fish to arrive at an unbiased estimate of concrete survival. At Little Goose Dam in 2009, this was not an issue, because the diel differences in survival were small; however, this may not always be the case. If tagged fish are released in appropriate number, time, and place to result in enough fish approaching and passing the dam during the day and night to estimate diel passage and survival parameters with acceptable precision, then these data can be weighted by the diel passage proportions of untagged fish to arrive at an overall estimate of concrete survival. This weighting would not be required if estimates of survival were similar for fish passing during the day and night.

There is uncertainty about what constitutes meeting the Biological Opinion survival standards (National Oceanic and Atmospheric Administration National Marine Fisheries Service, 2008). There are many methods to estimate survival parameters. These include the capture-recapture models themselves (for example, RSSM, other paired-release, or single-release models) as well as how estimates from them are determined, as there are many variations in how the models can be formed and evaluated. In this study, we evaluated a series of models to determine which model parameters should be separately estimated and which could be assumed equal based on parsimony. We followed this with final models from which to estimate the parameters of interest. Parsimony rests on a balance between precision and bias. Precision degrades as the number of parameters increases and bias improves under these conditions: the goal is to balance these to achieve acceptable bias and precision (Burnham and Anderson, 2002). This approach often can be improved by model-averaging all models in the suite considered and making estimates of the parameters of interest from the model-averaged result. This approach incorporates model-selection uncertainty in the results, which has rarely been done for studies in the Columbia River Basin. One exception is the report of passage and survival at McNary Dam in 2007 by Adams and Counihan (2009). The approach is based on the realization that inferences based on a single model may ignore other important hypotheses supported by the data. One example is the use of a model to separately estimate passage and survival parameters of fish in each of two treatments when the data do not support a difference between treatments. The parsimony and model-averaging approaches commonly are used in other fields of biological research and are described in detail by Burnham and Anderson (2002).

Having established minimum survival mandates through the Biological Opinion (National Oceanic and Atmospheric Administration National Marine Fisheries Service, 2008) creates a need for improvements in the methods used for estimating survival. The most obvious may be the development of a new mark-recapture design. The model we have been using (RSSM; Skalski and others, 2002) does not have a provision for assessing post-release mortality of fish, which can theoretically create a biased estimate of the relative survival of treatment and control fish. Skalski (2009) developed a model to address this concern and it was implemented at The Dalles Dam on the Columbia River during 2010 (data were being processed at the time of this report). A regional change to a common telemetry system and field methods was underway as this report was completed. Additional scrutiny also is being placed on within-model methods used to estimate survival, such as comparing estimates from fish tagged by different people and empirical assessments of model assumptions.

Less obvious issues also should be addressed if the goal is to compare estimates of survival to a standard. This type of use treats the results as measures of absolute survival rather than survival for comparisons among treatments or routes within a study. If the data are to be used as estimates of absolute survival, then the consistency of methods used among studies needs more scrutiny than in the past. The issue of model selection uncertainty is important to consider in model development and use. For example, should all recapture probabilities be estimated separately, or can some be estimated together, reducing the number of estimated parameters and potentially increasing precision? What is the decision point for throwing out data from a particular person tagging fish—a statistically different estimate of survival? If so, how is that estimate to be made—from a single model, or will model selection uncertainty be included? These and other issues will require consideration if the results of studies estimating survival relative to a specific standard are to be comparable.

In summary, the operation of the dam with the low-crest TSW during 30% 24-h spill resulted in low probabilities of turbine passage, low probabilities of passage through conventional spill bays, high probabilities of TSW passage, and high concrete survival. The TSW was the most common route of passage, which is likely a result of the advantages inherent in surface passage devices plus its placement in an area known to have high passage rates in prior years. The estimates of concrete survival from yearling Chinook salmon, juvenile steelhead, and subyearling Chinook salmon met the precision goal and were greater than the minimum survivals mandated by the current Biological Opinion (National Oceanic and Atmospheric Administration National Marine Fisheries Service, 2008).

Acknowledgments

We thank Fred Higginbotham, Chris Pinney, George Melanson, and others in the U.S. Army Corps of Engineers for their cooperation and assistance on the project. We are especially grateful to Pat Keniry and Annie Dowdy and individuals in the Oregon Department of Fish and Wildlife for their assistance in collecting fish. We thank our colleagues at the Columbia River Research Laboratory for their assistance and dedication. The report was improved with comments from four reviewers. Funding for this project was provided by the U.S. Army Corps of Engineers, Walla Walla District, Washington, Contract W68SBV83256266.

References Cited

Adams, N.S., Rondorf, D.W., Evans, S.D., Kelly, J.E., and Perry, R.W., 1998, Effects of surgically and gastrically implanted radio transmitters on growth and feeding behavior of juvenile Chinook salmon: Transactions of the American Fisheries Society, v. 127, p.128–136.

Adams, N.S., and Counihan, T.D., eds., 2009, Survival and migration behavior of juvenile salmonids at McNary Dam, 2007: Final report of research prepared by U.S. Geological Survey, Cook, Washington, for the U.S. Army Corps of Engineers, Walla Walla District, Washington, Contract W68SBV70178419, Walla Walla, Washington.

Allison, P.D., 1995, Survival Analysis Using SAS®: A Practical Guide: Cary, North Carolina, SAS Institute Inc., 292 p.

Axel, G.A., Hockersmith, E.E., Ogden, D.A., Burke, B.J., Frick, K.E., and Sandford, B.P., 2007, Passage behavior and survival for radio-tagged yearling Chinook salmon and steelhead at Ice Harbor Dam, 2005: Final report of research prepared by the National Oceanic and Atmospheric Administration National Marine Fisheries Service, Pasco, Washington, for the U.S. Army Corps of Engineers, Walla Walla District, Washington, Contract W68SBV92844866, Walla Walla, Washington.

Beeman, J.W., Braatz, A.C., Fielding, S.D., Hansel, H.C., Brown, S.T., George, G.T., Haner, P.V., Hansen, G.S., and Shurtleff, D.J., 2008a, Approach, passage, and survival of juvenile salmonids at Little Goose Dam, 2007: Final report of research by the U.S. Geological Survey, Cook, Washington, for the U.S. Army Corps of Engineers, Walla Walla District, Washington, Contract W68SBV60317747, Walla Walla, Washington.

Beeman, J.W., Braatz, A.C., Fielding, S.D., Hardiman, J.M., Walker, C.E., Pope, A.C., Wilkerson, T.S., Shurtleff, D.J., Perry, R.W., and Counihan, T.D., 2008b, Passage, survival, and approach patterns of radio-tagged juvenile salmonids at Little Goose Dam, 2006: Final report of research prepared by the U.S. Geological Survey, Cook, Washington, for the U.S. Army Corps of Engineers, Walla Walla District, Washington, Contract W68SBV60317747, Walla Walla, Washington.

Beeman, J.W., Grant, C., and Haner, P.V., 2004, Comparison of three underwater antennas for use in radio telemetry: North American Journal of Fisheries Management, v. 24, p. 275–281.

Beeman, J.W., and Maule, A.G., 2006; Migration depths of juvenile Chinook salmon and steelhead relative to total dissolved gas supersaturation in a Columbia River reservoir: Transactions of the American Fisheries Society, v. 135, p. 584–594.

Burnham, K.P., Anderson, D.R., White, G.C., Brownie, C., and Pollock, K.H., 1987, Design and analysis methods for fish survival experiments based on release-recapture: Bethesda, Maryland, American Fisheries Society, America Fisheries Society Monograph 5, 737 p.

Burnham, K.P., and Anderson, D.R., 2002, Model selection and multimodel inference: A practical information-theoretic approach: New York, New York, Springer-Verlag, 488 p.

Cash, K.M., and others, 2005, Three-dimensional behavior and passage of juvenile salmonids at The Dalles Dam, 2004: Final report of research by the U.S. Geological Survey, Cook, Washington, and Battelle-Pacific Northwest Division, Richland, Washington, for the U.S. Army Corps of Engineers, Portland District, Oregon, Contract W66QKZ40278562, Portland, Oregon.

Castro-Santos, T., and Haro, A., 2003, Quantifying migratory delay: a new application of survival analysis methods: Canadian Journal of Fisheries and Aquatic Sciences, v. 60, p. 986–996.

Cormack, R.M., 1964, Estimates of survival from the sighting of marked animals: Biometrika, v. 51, no. 3/4, p. 429–438.

Cowen, L., and Schwarz, C.J., 2005, Capture-recapture studies using radio telemetry with premature radio-tag failure: Biometrics, v. 61, p. 657–664.

Fish Passage Center, 2010, Fish Passage Center website, accessed June 30, 2010, at http://www.fpc.org/.

Ham, K.D., Tizler, P.S., and Arimescu, C.L.L., 2009, Hydroacoustic evaluation of fish passage distributions at the removable spillway weir at Lower Monumental Dam in 2009: Report prepared by Battelle-Pacific Northwest Division, Richland, Washington, for U.S. Army Corps of Engineers, Walla Walla District, Washington, Contract W912EF-08-D-0004, Walla Walla, Washington.

Haro, A., Odeh, M., Noreika, J., and Castro-Santos, T., 1998, Effect of water acceleration on downstream migratory behavior and passage of Atlantic salmon smolts and juvenile American shad at surface bypasses: Transactions of the American Fisheries Society, v. 127, p. 118–127.

Hosmer, D.W., Jr., and Lemeshow, S., 1999, Applied survival analysis: regression modeling of time to event data: New York, John Wiley and Sons.

Jepson, M.A., Caudill, C.C., Clabough, T.S., Peery, C.A., Beeman, J.W., and Fielding, S.D., 2009, Adult Chinook salmon passage at Little Goose Dam in relation to spill operations, 2008: Report of research by Idaho Cooperative Fish and Wildlife Research Unit, University of Idaho, Moscow, Idaho, and U.S. Geological Survey, Cook, Washington, for the U.S. Army Corps of Engineers, Walla Walla District, Washington, Contract W68SBV80164718, Walla Walla, Washington.

Johnson, G.E., Adams, N.A., Johnson, R.L., Rondorf, D.W., Dauble, D.D., and Barila, T.L., 2000, Evaluation of the prototype surface bypass for salmonid smolts in spring 1996 and 1997 at Lower Granite Dam on the Snake River, Washington: Transactions of the American Fisheries Society, v. 129, p. 381–397.

Johnson, G.E., Sullivan, C.M., and Erho, M.W., 1992, Hydroacoustic studies for developing a smolt bypass system at Wells Dam: Fisheries Research, v.14, p. 221–237.

Jolly, G.M., 1965, Explicit estimates from capture-recapture data with both death and immigration-stochastic model: Biometrika, v. 52, no. 1/2, p. 225–247.

Lady, J.M., and Skalski, J.R., 2009, USER 4: User-specified estimation routine: Prepared for U.S. Department of Energy, Bonneville Power Administration, Portland, Oregon, Project No. 198910700, Portland, Oregon.

Lebreton, J.D., Burnham, K.P., Clobert, J., and Anderson, D.R., 1992, Modeling survival and testing biological hypotheses using marked animals: A unified approach with case studies: Ecological Monographs, v. 62, p. 67–118.

National Oceanic and Atmospheric Administration's National Marine Fisheries Service, 2008, Endangered Species Act Section 7(a)(2) Consultation Biological Opinion and Magnuson-Stevens Fishery Conservation and Management Act Essential Fish Habitat Consultation: NOAA, Log number F/NWR/2005/05883.

Normandeau Associates, Skalski, J.R., and Townsend, R., 2008, Direct injury and survival of juvenile Chinook salmon passing through the removable spillway weir (RSW) at Lower Monumental Dam, 2008: Report prepared by Normandeau Associates, Inc., Drumore, Pennsylvania, and University of Washington, Seattle, Washington, for the U.S. Army Corps of Engineers, Walla Walla District, Washington, Contract W912EF-08-D-0005, Walla Walla, Washington.

Normandeau Associates, Skalski, J.R., and Townsend, R., 2009, Estimates of injury and survival of juvenile Chinook salmon passing through a spillway equipped with a temporary spillway weir and a spillway with a new spill deflector at Little Goose Dam, 2009: Report prepared by Normandeau Associates, Inc. and Drumore, Pennsylvania, and University of Washington, Seattle, Washington, for the U.S. Army Corps of Engineers, Walla Walla District, Washington, Contract W912EF-08-D-0005, Walla Walla, Washington.

Ogden, D.A., Hockersmith, E.E., Eppard, M.B., Axel, G.A., and Sanford, B.P., 2005, Passage behavior and survival for river-run subyearling Chinook salmon at Ice Harbor Dam, 2004: Final report of research prepared by the National Oceanic and Atmospheric Administration National Marine Fisheries Service, Pasco, Washington, for the U.S. Army Corps of Engineers, Walla Walla District, Washington, Contract W68SBV92844866, Walla Walla, Washington.

Pacific States Marine Fisheries Commission, n.d, PIT tag information system for the Columbia River Basin: Fisheries Data Project, accessed June 30, 2010, at http://www.ptagis.org/ptagis/index.jsp.

Perry, R.W., Kock, T.J., Novick, M.S., Braatz, A.C., Fielding, S.D., Hansen, G.S., Sprando, J.M., Wilkerson, T.S., George, G.T., Schei, J.L., Adams, N.S., and Rondorf, D.W., 2007, Survival and migration behavior of juvenile salmonids at Lower Granite Dam, 2005: Final report of research by the U.S. Geological Survey, Cook, Washington, for the U.S. Army Corps of Engineers, Walla Walla District, Washington, Contract W68SBV50498133, Walla Walla, Washington.

Seber, G.A.F., 1965, A note on the multiple recapture census: Biometrika, v. 52, no.1/2. p. 249–259.

Seber, G.A.F., 1982, The estimation of animal abundance and related parameters: New York, New York, Macmillan, 654 p.

Skalski, J.R., Lady, J., Townsend, R., Giorgi, A.E., Stevenson, J.R., Peven, C.M., and McDonald, R.D., 2001, Estimating in-river survival of migrating salmonid smolts using radio-telemetry: Canadian Journal of Fisheries and Aquatic Sciences, v. 58, p. 1887–1997.

Skalski, J.R., Townsend, R., Lady, J., Giorgi, A.E., Stevenson, J.R., and McDonald, R.S., 2002, Estimating route-specific passage and survival probabilities at a hydroelectric project from smolt radiotelemetry studies: Canadian Journal of Fisheries and Aquatic Sciences, v. 59, p. 1385–1393.

Skalski, J.R., 2009, Statistical design for the lower Columbia River acoustic-tag investigations of dam passage survival and associated metrics, 19 May 2009: Report prepared by University of Washington, Seattle, Washington, for the U.S. Army Corps of Engineers, Portland, Oregon.

Swan, G.A., Eppard, M.B., Hockersmith, E.E., Sandford, B.P., Iverson, B.L., Ocker, P.A., Kaminski, M.A., and Iwamoto, R.N., 1995, Juvenile radio-telemetry study at Ice Harbor Dam, 1995: Annual report of research prepared by the National Oceanic and Atmospheric Administration National Marine Fisheries Service, Pasco, Washington, for the U.S. Army Corps of Engineers, Walla Walla, Washington.

Townsend, R.L., Skalski, J.R., Dillingham, P., and Steig, T.W., 2006, Correcting bias in survival estimation resulting from tag failure in acoustic and radiotelemetry studies: Journal of Agricultural, Biological, and Environmental Statistics, v. 11, p. 183–196.

University of Washington, 2010, Columbia River DART website, accessed June 30, 2010, at http://www.cbr.washington.edu/dart/dart.html.

U.S. Navy, n.d., Naval Oceanography Portal website, accessed June 30, 2010, at http://www.usno.navy.mil/USNO/astronomical-applications/data-services.

Zabel, R.W., 1994, Spatial and temporal models of migrating juvenile salmon with applications: Seattle, University of Washington, Ph.D. dissertation.

Zabel, R.W., and Anderson, J.J., 1997, A model of the travel time of migrating juvenile salmon, with an application to Snake River spring Chinook salmon: North American Journal of Fisheries Management, v. 17, p. 93–100.

Glossary

CH0	Hatchery and wild Subyearling Chinook salmon *Oncorhynchus tshawytscha*)
CH1	Hatchery yearling Chinook salmon (*O. tshawytscha*)
Forebay	Area of Snake River from Little Goose Dam to 2 km upstream.
HST	Hatchery steelhead (*O. mykiss*).
PIT	Passive integrated transponder.
Powerhouse	Turbine and Bypass (units 1–6).
RKM	River kilometer.
Spillway	Conventional spill bays (bays 2–8).
NOAA Fisheries	National Oceanic and Atmospheric Administration National Marine Fisheries Service.
Tailrace	Area of Snake River from Little Goose Dam to 1.4 km downstream.
TSW	Temporary Spillway Weir.
USACE	United States Army Corps of Engineers.
USGS	United States Geological Survey.

Appendix A. Fish Release Summaries

Table A1. Descriptive statistics of fork length and weight by release date and release group of yearling Chinook salmon radio-tagged and released to estimate route-specific survival at Little Goose Dam, spring 2009.

| Release | | Release | | Fork Length (mm) | | | Weight (g) | | |
Date	Time	group	N	Mean	SD	Range	Mean	SD	Range
18-Apr	11:43:06	Treatment	28	139.7	15.0	120 – 170	28.9	10.2	16.9 – 52.1
19-Apr	14:40:06	Treatment	24	144.1	14.8	119 – 179	31.0	8.5	15.2 – 51.0
19-Apr	11:23:47	Control	16	134.4	7.6	121 – 145	26.1	5.0	16.4 – 32.1
20-Apr	21:17:41	Treatment	28	143.3	18.0	117 – 195	32.2	12.7	14.8 – 70.3
20-Apr	18:24:48	Control	18	140.5	14.1	119 – 167	30.7	9.6	16.5 – 47.2
21-Apr	18:42:30	Treatment	27	137.6	12.9	118 – 160	27.5	8.4	14.6 – 46.2
21-Apr	21:55:16	Control	18	137.6	14.8	114 – 166	26.9	9.2	14.3 – 44.2
22-Apr	13:15:46	Treatment	25	140.0	11.8	118 – 166	29.0	7.4	17.2 – 42.9
22-Apr	10:34:27	Control	17	135.9	10.4	122 – 155	25.4	6.0	18.8 – 36.0
23-Apr	11:09:06	Treatment	28	133.9	12.2	118 – 170	25.1	8.2	15.3 – 47.5
23-Apr	14:03:47	Control	18	136.7	12.4	119 – 165	25.9	7.5	16.0 – 39.9
24-Apr	18:00:37	Treatment	29	135.5	13.4	115 – 163	26.2	8.4	16.0 – 43.3
24-Apr	20:58:51	Control	17	131.4	9.9	118 – 146	23.5	5.9	14.6 – 31.2
25-Apr	21:06:50	Treatment	28	139.8	12.1	115 – 165	27.9	6.9	16.7 – 43.3
25-Apr	17:57:20	Control	19	143.5	13.4	119 – 169	30.9	8.4	16.6 – 47.9
26-Apr	10:14:37	Treatment	27	140.6	12.7	119 – 164	28.0	7.9	16.2 – 45.4
26-Apr	13:41:02	Control	18	138.6	9.6	124 – 155	26.6	6.1	17.6 – 40.5
27-Apr	12:50:25	Treatment	25	148.2	9.3	129 – 168	33.4	6.2	21.7 – 49.2
27-Apr	9:59:03	Control	18	143.2	16.1	122 – 169	30.7	10.5	17.3 – 49.5
28-Apr	21:00:00	Treatment	27	144.2	10.3	118 – 167	30.2	6.3	15.3 – 44.0
28-Apr	17:55:43	Control	18	144.5	14.5	120 – 179	31.2	9.7	16.2 – 53.4
29-Apr	18:01:17	Treatment	28	138.7	13.1	119 – 175	26.8	8.2	15.9 – 51.2
29-Apr	21:47:47	Control	18	143.7	11.9	123 – 165	29.7	7.7	16.6 – 42.5
30-Apr	10:17:58	Treatment	28	141.1	10.1	124 – 162	28.6	6.5	16.8 – 45.0
30-Apr	13:11:19	Control	19	134.6	11.3	115 – 153	24.5	6.2	15.0 – 33.7
1-May	13:07:38	Treatment	25	135.0	10.7	117 – 154	23.5	6.9	14.4 – 41.4
1-May	10:41:05	Control	17	143.3	12.5	126 – 163	29.8	7.8	18.6 – 43.3
2-May	18:04:04	Treatment	27	137.8	12.4	119 – 172	25.9	7.7	16.3 – 48.1
2-May	21:07:28	Control	19	137.8	10.6	122 – 159	26.2	7.6	16.6 – 46.3
3-May	20:48:23	Treatment	28	141.3	12.3	126 – 171	28.2	8.5	18.2 – 51.2
3-May	17:45:07	Control	19	133.8	11.2	117 – 152	24.0	7.1	14.9 – 36.1
4-May	12:52:24	Treatment	25	137.9	10.0	126 – 159	25.7	6.3	17.9 – 38.7
4-May	10:23:43	Control	16	136.8	10.9	120 – 163	26.0	7.0	17.6 – 45.5
5-May	10:41:50	Treatment	28	135.2	9.2	119 – 153	23.6	4.8	15.6 – 33.9
5-May	13:46:10	Control	18	139.5	10.2	122 – 160	27.7	7.6	17.0 – 49.6
6-May	21:50:20	Treatment	27	139.6	11.5	125 – 166	26.4	7.1	18.8 – 44.2
6-May	18:17:32	Control	18	141.2	7.7	130 – 159	27.8	4.7	20.5 – 39.6
7-May	18:22:30	Treatment	28	137.8	11.8	121 – 166	25.6	7.4	15.5 – 45.8
7-May	21:18:28	Control	18	145.8	12.5	127 – 170	30.0	7.3	19.1 – 46.7
8-May	10:19:28	Treatment	28	136.9	10.5	121 – 157	24.6	6.1	16.3 – 35.7

Table A1 continued.

Release		Release		Fork Length (mm)			Weight (g)		
Date	Time	group	N	Mean	SD	Range	Mean	SD	Range
8-May	13:14:12	Control	19	142.8	10.4	125 – 161	27.8	6.9	17.3 – 42.1
9-May	10:26:30	Treatment	27	140.1	9.0	120 – 155	26.3	5.2	14.8 – 37.2
9-May	13:48:01	Control	18	137.1	11.6	110 – 155	24.6	6.0	14.3 – 35.6
10-May	21:00:20	Treatment	27	140.3	8.8	118 – 156	26.0	5.3	14.6 – 36.9
10-May	18:03:44	Control	19	140.2	8.9	124 – 156	26.1	5.4	18.7 – 37.4
11-May	18:20:06	Treatment	26	137.9	9.4	121 – 156	24.7	5.6	16.7 – 38.1
11-May	21:20:53	Control	19	132.3	6.8	120 –148	21.7	3.4	15.7 – 30.9
12-May	13:05:39	Treatment	24	133.8	7.1	122 – 147	22.1	3.6	15.1 – 29.8
12-May	10:19:19	Control	17	133.4	9.8	120 – 161	22.2	5.1	16.5 – 37.8
13-May	13:05:08	Treatment	25	137.8	8.2	123 – 152	24.2	5.0	15.8 – 34.2
13-May	10:05:47	Control	16	143.0	8.6	126 – 155	28.3	5.7	18.0 – 38.3
14-May	17:57:06	Treatment	28	140.0	9.4	119 – 153	26.4	5.4	16.0 – 36.8
14-May	21:19:50	Control	18	133.6	10.4	119 – 151	22.5	6.0	15.3 – 36.1
15-May	18:05:12	Treatment	27	140.8	7.8	123 – 157	26.5	5.1	16.3 – 38.0
15-May	20:58:20	Control	18	135.8	7.5	125 – 156	23.1	3.9	17.8 – 34.9
16-May	13:04:56	Treatment	24	136.9	6.7	127 – 149	24.3	4.5	18.7 – 39.2
16-May	10:17:52	Control	17	140.9	6.5	130 – 150	26.3	6.5	19.7 – 34.8
17-May	10:16:24	Treatment	27	142.3	7.5	129 - 162	27.4	5.0	20.1 – 40.8
17-May	13:32:27	Control	18	143.8	6.6	135 – 152	28.1	4.3	21.0 – 34.6
18-May	21:05:40	Treatment	28	138.8	7.1	125 – 156	24.9	4.4	18.6 – 36.7
18-May	17:57:44	Control	19	141.7	7.8	128 – 160	27.1	4.8	18.2 – 38.4
19-May	21:09:31	Treatment	26	139.5	6.8	125 – 153	25.4	3.7	16.5 – 31.3
19-May	18:08:11	Control	18	139.4	7.3	124 – 148	25.3	3.8	17.3 – 29.9
20-May	13:30:41	Treatment	26	139.5	9.6	121 – 160	25.0	5.4	17.4 – 39.3
20-May	10:21:20	Control	16	143.3	22.9	125 – 226	24.1	3.8	18.1 – 31.1
21-May	12:38:15	Control	16	139.7	5.6	129 – 151	26.0	3.6	20.1 – 34.4

Table A2. Descriptive statistics of fork length and weight by release date and release group of juvenile steelhead radio-tagged and released to estimate route-specific survival, Little Goose Dam, spring 2009.

Release		Release		Fork Length (mm)			Weight (g)		
Date	Time	group	N	Mean	SD	Range	Mean	SD	Range
18-Apr	11:43:06	Treatment	28	223.8	19.6	182 – 255	104.2	24.9	59.0 – 144.3
19-Apr	14:40:06	Treatment	28	219.3	18.7	176 – 250	97.6	26.5	50.8 – 144.4
19-Apr	11:23:47	Control	16	228.2	17.3	208 – 270	111.6	32.0	81.7 – 196.0
20-Apr	21:17:41	Treatment	20	227.1	21.2	196 – 265	110.6	32.2	60.5 – 169.3
20-Apr	18:24:48	Control	14	227.8	15.1	204 – 258	110.9	25.3	78.8 – 162.9
21-Apr	18:42:30	Treatment	33	226.3	17.6	180 – 262	109.7	25.5	57.7 – 166.4
21-Apr	21:55:16	Control	21	223.0	15.5	205 – 264	103.1	25.2	74.0 – 173.9
22-Apr	13:15:46	Treatment	25	210.7	16.7	175 – 235	87.0	22.1	45.8 – 138.6
22-Apr	10:34:27	Control	17	203.8	14.3	179 – 235	78.8	19.8	47.1 – 128.0
23-Apr	11:09:06	Treatment	28	200.5	13.9	166 – 241	74.3	15.1	44.3 – 126.0
23-Apr	14:03:47	Control	18	206.3	13.9	183 – 235	80.1	18.9	56.5 – 131.8
24-Apr	18:00:37	Treatment	28	204.3	13.7	178 – 243	78.2	16.4	51.6 – 126.6

Table A2 continued.

| Release | | Release | | Fork Length (mm) | | | Weight (g) | | |
Date	Time	group	N	Mean	SD	Range	Mean	SD	Range
24-Apr	20:58:51	Control	19	203.4	18.1	179 – 242	77.7	22.5	53.0 – 129.7
25-Apr	21:06:50	Treatment	28	199.6	10.3	183 – 214	70.7	10.5	52.4 – 94.0
25-Apr	17:57:20	Control	19	194.4	9.2	179 – 210	65.4	9.0	50.8 – 84.3
26-Apr	10:14:37	Treatment	27	197.6	11.8	168 – 221	69.1	10.4	43.3 – 90.4
26-Apr	13:41:02	Control	18	196.2	12.5	161 – 213	66.8	13.0	33.2 – 87.1
27-Apr	12:50:25	Treatment	24	192.1	11.5	165 – 211	62.0	10.7	41.1 – 83.1
27-Apr	9:59:03	Control	16	195.6	12.6	166 – 218	67.6	12.3	42.7 – 91.4
28-Apr	21:00:00	Treatment	27	206.0	17.2	163 – 237	78.2	19.0	36.8 – 115.8
28-Apr	17:55:43	Control	18	209.6	18.8	167 – 245	84.2	23.7	42.9 – 136.6
29-Apr	18:01:17	Treatment	28	189.2	18.5	137 – 216	59.5	15.3	19.7 – 89.6
29-Apr	21:47:47	Control	16	192.8	17.3	155 – 213	62.9	17.2	29.5 – 91.0
30-Apr	10:17:58	Treatment	28	211.8	18.7	184 – 250	88.3	25.3	56.3 – 144.3
30-Apr	13:11:19	Control	18	202.9	16.1	173 – 225	75.8	16.1	42.4 – 105.2
1-May	13:07:38	Treatment	24	215.5	19.2	180 – 250	89.4	26.2	48.2 – 138.2
1-May	10:41:05	Control	17	213.4	19.0	175 – 252	90.2	28.7	45.0 – 152.3
2-May	18:04:04	Treatment	27	218.1	19.5	181 – 260	94.9	26.4	51.6 – 157.0
2-May	21:07:28	Control	20	214.4	19.9	184 – 275	89.6	30.2	54.9 – 190.0
3-May	20:48:23	Treatment	28	209.0	12.9	186 – 232	81.7	16.8	55.5 – 113.3
3-May	17:45:07	Control	19	218.4	15.6	186 – 239	92.5	19.4	58.9 – 127.0
4-May	12:52:24	Treatment	25	210.0	14.5	187 – 238	82.0	19.2	54.1 – 125.2
4-May	10:23:43	Control	16	215.1	20.2	175 – 241	89.9	25.4	44.8 – 131.2
5-May	10:41:50	Treatment	28	206.8	20.8	172 – 255	78.7	24.4	46.2 – 137.0
5-May	13:46:10	Control	19	208.3	19.3	170 – 237	82.3	25.9	41.3 – 130.3
6-May	21:50:20	Treatment	28	217.8	21.6	152 – 253	94.5	27.5	29.7 – 152.6
6-May	18:17:32	Control	18	220.2	17.7	190 – 246	97.7	24.7	57.1 – 138.4
7-May	18:22:30	Treatment	28	227.6	16.9	200 – 259	105.5	26.5	70.1 – 154.1
7-May	21:18:28	Control	18	224.4	19.2	180 – 249	97.5	23.5	52.6 – 127.5
8-May	10:19:28	Treatment	28	224.2	19.9	186 – 259	100.9	28.7	63.4 – 162.9
8-May	13:14:12	Control	19	213.2	20.9	181 – 254	84.6	24.1	54.3 – 144.6
9-May	10:26:30	Treatment	27	217.1	19.0	168 – 248	89.9	25.4	36.5 – 136.2
9-May	13:48:01	Control	18	220.8	21.3	181 – 260	96.3	31.5	45.8 – 165.3
10-May	21:00:20	Treatment	27	210.1	18.7	175 – 240	83.3	24.3	41.8 – 132.3
10-May	18:03:44	Control	19	224.1	19.3	194 – 259	101.9	29.8	60.6 – 165.1
11-May	18:20:06	Treatment	28	222.3	19.6	179 – 259	95.6	27.4	52.2 – 149.7
11-May	21:20:53	Control	19	223.1	15.3	193 – 254	98.5	20.6	57.3 – 134.1
12-May	13:05:39	Treatment	24	215.6	15.1	181 – 240	87.3	19.7	50.0 – 123.9
12-May	10:19:19	Control	17	221.6	17.4	175 – 250	96.4	22.7	42.3 – 126.1
13-May	13:05:08	Treatment	25	228.5	26.5	179 – 275	106.6	41.5	42.1 – 182.2
13-May	10:05:47	Control	16	229.4	15.0	204 – 252	105.5	21.7	74.0 – 139.4
14-May	17:57:06	Treatment	28	227.7	22.8	185 – 269	105.7	34.1	47.8 – 166.7
14-May	21:19:50	Control	18	232.5	22.8	193 – 284	114.6	39.1	61.5 – 216.4
15-May	18:05:12	Treatment	27	226.6	21.8	185 – 271	103.7	32.6	50.4 – 171.0
15-May	20:58:20	Control	18	211.3	16.5	184 – 243	83.0	22.3	54.8 – 128.7
16-May	13:04:56	Treatment	24	219.8	27.4	171 – 273	96.9	40.9	41.4 – 205.6
16-May	10:17:52	Control	16	225.9	19.2	190 – 269	102.5	30.0	60.3 – 185.5
17-May	10:16:24	Treatment	27	226.7	21.5	200 – 272	104.8	35.1	64.0 – 190.0
17-May	13:32:27	Control	18	222.5	21.6	184 – 275	94.9	28.4	53.0 – 171.8

Table A2 continued.

Release		Release		Fork Length (mm)			Weight (g)		
Date	Time	group	N	Mean	SD	Range	Mean	SD	Range
18-May	21:05:40	Treatment	27	213.2	24.2	154 – 250	82.8	27.2	30.4 – 135.6
18-May	17:57:44	Control	17	218.0	21.6	178 – 247	91.9	29.5	45.9 – 136.0
19-May	21:09:31	Treatment	25	226.7	29.9	145 – 273	104.0	38.2	25.7 – 176.3
19-May	18:08:11	Control	18	220.9	25.9	182 – 274	97.3	37.2	48.9 – 188.2
20-May	13:30:41	Treatment	23	226.4	23.6	171 – 268	102.3	32.8	37.2 – 172.1
20-May	10:21:20	Control	18	236.2	17.7	208 – 269	112.5	26.6	72.0 – 164.6
21-May	12:38:15	Control	19	211.5	24.1	165 – 258	80.2	31.6	34.1 – 149.9

Table A3. Descriptive statistics of fork length and weight by release date and release group of subyearling Chinook salmon radio-tagged and released to estimate route-specific survival at Little Goose Dam, summer 2009.

Release		Release		Fork Length (mm)			Weight (g)		
Date	Time	group	N	Mean	SD	Range	Mean	SD	Range
6-Jun	11:16:41	Treatment	96	105.9	3.1	99 – 116	11.6	1.1	10.0 – 14.9
7-Jun	13:02:53	Treatment	67	106.3	4.0	100 – 117	11.6	1.4	10.0 – 16.4
7-Jun	10:03:23	Control	60	106.3	4.0	100 – 119	11.7	1.5	10.0 – 17.5
8-Jun	17:55:25	Treatment	38	106.2	4.3	100 – 117	11.5	1.4	10.0 – 15.2
8-Jun	21:02:37	Control	18	107.3	4.6	100 – 120	11.9	1.6	10.2 – 16.8
9-Jun	21:08:00	Treatment	117	107.1	4.2	101 – 121	11.9	1.4	10.0 – 17.1
9-Jun	17:33:17	Control	60	107.4	4.6	101 – 119	12.1	1.6	10.0 – 16.3
10-Jun	10:28:05	Treatment	102	105.9	4.3	98 – 118	11.7	1.5	10.0 – 16.7
10-Jun	13:50:50	Control	42	106.6	4.0	100 – 117	11.7	1.3	10.0 – 14.7
11-Jun	13:06:14	Treatment	72	106.9	4.3	100 – 125	12.0	1.7	10.2 – 20.6
11-Jun	10:15:29	Control	46	107.6	4.7	100 – 119	12.4	1.8	10.2 – 17.6
12-Jun	17:25:51	Treatment	54	106.9	4.2	100 – 119	12.1	1.6	10.0 – 16.3
12-Jun	20:57:25	Control	37	106.4	4.3	97 – 118	11.7	1.3	10.2 – 14.6
13-Jun	21:20:13	Treatment	65	106.8	4.9	99 – 118	12.1	1.8	10.0 – 17.7
13-Jun	17:52:12	Control	44	107.2	4.2	98 – 117	12.3	1.6	10.0 – 17.7
14-Jun	12:53:23	Treatment	24	105.9	3.8	99 – 112	11.7	1.2	10.0 – 13.5
14-Jun	10:36:03	Control	19	106.3	4.4	99 – 114	11.9	1.4	10.0 – 14.4
15-Jun	10:04:58	Treatment	48	109.1	6.4	100 – 126	13.2	2.6	10.4 – 21.7
15-Jun	13:00:38	Control	32	106.8	6.2	100 – 125	12.4	2.4	10.0 – 20.3
16-Jun	21:13:53	Treatment	116	107.2	5.4	96 – 125	12.3	1.9	10.0 – 18.3
16-Jun	17:46:28	Control	68	107.9	5.5	99 – 121	12.5	2.0	10.0 – 17.8
17-Jun	18:16:20	Treatment	118	108.3	6.9	96 – 142	12.7	3.0	10.0 – 32.3
17-Jun	21:40:18	Control	69	107.5	5.8	99 – 128	12.1	2.0	10.0 – 18.8
18-Jun	13:24:02	Treatment	108	107.4	4.9	99 – 121	12.1	1.8	10.0 – 19.7
18-Jun	10:17:15	Control	70	107.3	5.4	99 – 120	12.2	1.8	10.0 – 17.3
19-Jun	13:38:03	Treatment	108	107.7	4.8	99 – 121	12.4	1.9	10.0 – 20.8
19-Jun	10:20:55	Control	70	108.1	5.8	99 – 126	12.6	2.3	10.0 – 21.0
20-Jun	21:18:51	Treatment	108	106.8	4.4	100 – 118	12.1	1.5	10.0 – 17.0
20-Jun	17:59:03	Control	70	106.8	5.1	99 – 121	12.0	1.8	10.0 – 18.0
21-Jun	18:31:37	Treatment	108	107.5	4.7	99 – 123	12.4	1.6	10.0 – 18.1
21-Jun	22:11:14	Control	70	107.4	5.3	100 – 127	12.2	2.0	10.0 – 21.8

Table A3 continued.

Release		Release		Fork Length (mm)			Weight (g)		
Date	Time	group	N	Mean	SD	Range	Mean	SD	Range
22-Jun	10:07:51	Treatment	106	105.7	3.8	100 – 119	11.8	1.5	10.0 – 18.4
22-Jun	13:27:57	Control	67	105.5	4.5	97 – 122	11.5	1.5	10.0 – 17.6
23-Jun	13:36:40	Treatment	102	105.2	3.5	100 – 119	11.6	1.3	10.0 – 17.0
23-Jun	10:36:30	Control	71	107.1	4.7	101 – 125	12.2	1.8	10.0 – 19.9
24-Jun	18:06:08	Treatment	107	107.1	5.2	98 – 123	12.5	2.1	10.0 – 20.1
24-Jun	21:14:14	Control	70	105.3	4.0	99 – 120	11.7	1.4	10.0 – 16.8
25-Jun	21:11:12	Treatment	118	105.2	4.5	98 – 124	11.7	1.6	10.0 – 18.4
25-Jun	18:01:40	Control	74	106.3	4.3	99 – 122	12.1	1.6	10.1 – 19.2
26-Jun	10:22:30	Treatment	79	105.9	5.8	97 – 125	12.0	2.2	10.0 – 19.5
26-Jun	13:26:50	Control	56	105.9	5.3	98 – 120	11.9	2.1	10.0 – 18.9
27-Jun	9:56:57	Treatment	47	106.7	5.6	99 – 120	12.3	2.1	10.0 – 18.5
27-Jun	13:14:12	Control	28	104.3	4.6	97 – 117	11.5	1.7	10.0 – 17.6
28-Jun	21:09:31	Treatment	55	105.8	4.8	97 – 118	12.4	1.9	10.0 – 17.7
28-Jun	17:56:40	Control	41	110.2	7.5	100 – 137	13.9	3.3	10.3 – 27.4
29-Jun	18:14:02	Treatment	120	109.3	7.2	99 – 133	13.6	3.1	10.0 – 26.0
29-Jun	21:38:24	Control	75	106.1	4.8	97 – 122	12.2	1.9	10.0 – 20.7
30-Jun	10:45:12	Treatment	122	108.1	7.1	99 – 135	13.3	3.2	10.0 – 27.8
30-Jun	13:51:54	Control	69	105.9	5.4	97 – 130	12.0	2.2	10.0 – 24.5
1-Jul	13:45:14	Treatment	103	106.3	5.8	98 – 133	12.2	2.5	10.0 – 27.2
1 - Jul	10:31:54	Control	60	107.8	8.5	98 – 142	12.9	4.2	10.0 – 34.5
2-Jul	18:15:42	Treatment	128	109.2	8.3	98 – 139	13.8	3.9	10.0 – 30.9
2-Jul	21:46:18	Control	69	106.5	5.5	97 – 123	12.5	2.5	10.0 – 22.2
3-Jul	22:04:00	Treatment	133	108.1	7.0	98 – 141	13.2	3.2	10.1 – 31.6
3-Jul	18:17:41	Control	64	106.8	6.8	98 – 127	12.7	2.9	10.0 – 25.3
4-Jul	11:57:12	Control	66	107.7	7.8	98 – 136	13.3	3.5	10.0 – 28.8
5-Jul	11:21:24	Control	47	111.3	9.0	98 – 134	15.2	4.4	10.0 – 28.5

Table A4. Descriptive statistics of radio-tagged yearling Chinook salmon fork length and weight by release date that were euthanized and released into the tailrace to estimate route-specific survival at Little Goose Dam, spring 2009.

Release			Fork Length (mm)			Weight (g)		
Date	Time	N	Mean	SD	Range	Mean	SD	Range
19-Apr	11:23:47	5	140.6	4.8	136 – 148	29.2	3.5	24.5 – 34.4
21-Apr	21:55:16	5	138.6	6.1	132 – 146	28.5	4.3	23.1 – 33.6
26-Apr	13:41:02	5	143.2	7.1	136 – 155	29.1	6.0	24.0 – 39.3
29-Apr	21:47:47	5	136.4	17.2	116 – 155	26.3	10.9	14.4 – 38.5
1-May	10:41:05	5	127.4	17.5	110 – 149	22.2	8.9	14.8 – 33.9
6-May	18:17:32	5	139.0	8.2	125 – 145	25.9	4.0	19.1 – 29.4
9-May	13:48:01	5	127.4	8.0	120 – 140	19.0	4.2	16.1 – 26.4
14-May	21:19:50	5	131.0	9.1	119 – 141	20.5	4.3	15.7 – 25.8
17-May	13:32:27	5	142.2	8.2	135 – 156	27.4	4.8	23.1 – 35.1
19-May	18:08:11	5	140.8	4.2	134 – 145	25.8	1.9	22.9 – 27.6

Table A5. Descriptive statistics of radio-tagged juvenile steelhead fork length and weight by release date that were euthanized and released into the tailrace to estimate route-specific survival at Little Goose Dam, spring 2009.

Release			Fork Length (mm)			Weight (g)		
Date	Time	N	Mean	SD	Range	Mean	SD	Range
19-Apr	11:23:47	5	225.2	21.2	200 – 255	105.5	37.1	68.8 – 161.0
21-Apr	21:55:16	5	224.2	10.2	208 – 236	102.7	13.2	86.0 – 116.5
26-Apr	13:41:02	5	199.6	18.2	173 – 223	71.5	16.9	47.1 – 90.7
29-Apr	21:47:47	5	190.6	18.9	172 – 218	59.6	15.8	44.9 – 82.2
1-May	10:41:05	5	224.6	16.6	206 – 248	106.2	24.6	78.0 – 140.6
6-May	18:17:32	5	231.0	15.2	219 – 253	112.1	24.9	92.3 – 150.7
9-May	13:48:01	5	232.4	11.8	214 – 243	109.8	19.3	81.3 – 128.3
14-May	21:19:50	5	215.0	12.8	196 – 229	85.3	22.1	58.2 – 111.3
17-May	13:32:27	5	235.8	23.0	207 – 271	112.9	36.9	75.9 – 173.6
19-May	18:08:11	5	220.4	30.9	180 – 259	102.0	41.3	54.7 – 153.5

Table A6. Descriptive statistics of radio-tagged subyearling Chinook salmon fork length and weight by release date that were euthanized and released into the tailrace to estimate route-specific survival at Little Goose Dam, summer 2009.

Release			Fork Length (mm)			Weight (g)		
Date	Time	N	Mean	SD	Range	Mean	SD	Range
8-Jun	21:02:37	5	105.6	4.4	101 – 112	11.0	1.2	10.2 – 13.2
10-Jun	13:50:50	5	106.8	2.6	104 – 110	11.9	0.6	10.9 – 12.5
12-Jun	20:57:25	5	112.6	9.3	103 – 128	14.5	3.9	10.6 – 20.9
14-Jun	10:36:03	5	105.4	1.1	104 – 107	12.3	1.2	11.3 – 14.3
17-Jun	21:40:18	5	107.4	7.9	101 – 121	12.1	3.2	10.2 – 17.7
19-Jun	10:20:55	5	107.2	4.6	103 – 114	12.0	1.2	10.9 – 13.8
22-Jun	13:27:57	5	109.0	2.6	105 – 112	12.9	1.0	11.5 – 13.9
25-Jun	18:01:40	5	107.6	8.8	101 – 123	13.2	3.8	10.5 – 19.9
29-Jun	21:38:24	5	106.0	6.1	100 – 114	12.0	1.9	10.1 – 14.5
1-Jul	10:31:54	5	109.6	12.9	100 – 132	14.0	6.5	10.2 – 25.6

Appendix B. Tag life

Introduction

A tag life study was conducted to test assumption 7 that all tags are correctly identified and marks are not lost during the study. In the case of radio telemetry, when a transmitter fails, the mark is essentially lost. Significant premature failure of transmitters can negatively bias survival estimates, because survival models will interpret tag failure as mortality. However, if the rate of tag failure is known, survival estimates can be adjusted to correct for tag failure (Cowen and Schwartz, 2005; Townsend and others, 2006). Therefore, it is important to conduct a tag life study as a measure of insurance. If a tag life study is not conducted, then little recourse is available for accurately adjusting survival estimates after conducting a study and finding that tags failed prematurely. Premature tag failure may occur through a number of mechanisms including batch-specific manufacturer defects or long travel times of fish because of low flows. Thus, it is important to conduct a tag life study using a random subsample of transmitters that will be implanted in fish and test their performance under ambient field conditions during the study period. The methods of Townsend and others (2006) were used to achieve the following goals of the tag life study: (1) to estimate the probability that a tag was alive at any point in time after it was turned on, (2) to estimate the probability of tags being in the study area at any given point in time after release, and (3) to estimate the average probability of a tag being alive when passing telemetry arrays used for survival analysis. Given this information, it was determined whether the tag failure rate was high enough to warrant correction of survival estimates.

Methods

The tag life study was conducted *in situ* during the spring and summer radio-tagged fish release periods at Little Goose Dam during 2009. Prior to conducting the tag life study, we randomly selected 50 model NTC-3-1 transmitters (used with yearling Chinook salmon and juvenile steelhead) and 50 model NTC-M-2 transmitters (used with subyearling Chinook salmon) from the tags to be used for the survival study. The tags were held in a large rectangular metal tank at the Little Goose Dam juvenile fish bypass facility and supplied with a constant flow of ambient river water. At the beginning of the spring and summer survival studies, one-third of the transmitters were turned on, the date and time was recorded, and the tags were placed inside 7.6 L galvanized steel buckets to prevent the radio signal from transmitting beyond the confines of the study area. Another one-third of the tags were turned on midway through the survival study, and the remaining tags were turned on at the date that coincided with the last fish release. Tags were monitored with a Lotek SRX data logging receiver until all tags ceased operation.

Next, we estimated the probability of a tag being alive at any given point in time. The lifetime of each tag was calculated as the elapsed time between the time a tag was turned on and the time that the last detection was recorded by the data logging receiver.

Any tag that ceased operation in less than 1 day was excluded from the analysis because we normally discover tags that malfunction within the 24-h recovery period of tagged fish. We then fit a survival distribution function to the tag life data to estimate the probability of a tag operating for a given amount of time. Although many forms of survival distribution functions can be fit to this data, we chose to use the Kaplan-Meier distribution because this distribution fits the tag life data well. The Kaplan-Meier survival distribution function takes the form

$$S(t) = Pr\{T>t\} \tag{B1}$$

where $S(t)$ is the probability of a tag surviving to time t. We used maximum likelihood methods to fit the Kaplan-Meier survival distribution function to the empirical survival distribution function. The empirical survival distribution function is simply the proportion of tags surviving to time t.

The probability that a tag is alive when it arrives at a detection array is dependent on the travel time of the tag to each detection array used in the survival analysis. For the route specific survival model, the travel times of interest are from time of release of the treatment group to the time of detection at Little Goose Dam, and from the release of both treatment and control groups to the time of first detection at any one of the downstream arrays used for survival analysis. In addition to fish travel time, the travel time of the tag must include all elapsed time that the transmitter was operating prior to fish release. Therefore, we recorded dates and times of all instances where transmitters were turned on or off, calculated the total elapsed time, and added this to the travel time of fish to each detection array. We then plotted the empirical cumulative travel time distribution, which is simply the proportion of fish arriving at a given detection array at time t, against the survival distribution function to understand whether most fish passed the detection arrays prior to tag failure.

To quantify the rate of tag failure we calculated the average probability that the tag was operational for the ith release group to the jth detection array (Townsend and others, 2006):

$$\hat{P}(L_{ij}) = \frac{1}{k_{ij}} \sum_{x=1}^{k_{ij}} \hat{S}(t_{ijx}) \tag{B2}$$

Where $\hat{P}(L_{ij})$ = average probability that a tag is alive at the jth detection array (1 = Little Goose Dam, 2 = first detection at the last downstream array) from the ith release group (1 = treatment released near Central Ferry State Park, Washington, 2 = control released in the Little Goose Dam tailrace).

$\hat{S}(h_{ijx})$ = the estimated probability that a tag is alive at time t_{ijx} for the xth fish arriving at the jth detection array for the ith release group. $\hat{S}(h_{ijx})$ is calculated simply by plugging into the survival distribution function the travel time of each tag to each detection array.

k_{ij} = the total number of fish detected at the jth detection array for the ith release group.

Results

The lifetime of most transmitters exceeded the minimum battery life of 16 days as specified by the manufacturer (appendix Fig. B1); however, two NTC-3-1 and six NTC-M-2 transmitters ceased operation prior to the manufacturer's specifications. Two NTC-3-1 and one NTC-M-2 ceased operation in less than 1 day and these transmitters were excluded from the analysis. The range of premature tag life failure was 4.8 to 15.3 days for the other five transmitters (fig. B1). The mean operational life time was 18.9 days for the NTC-3-1, and 22.1 days for the NTC-M-2 transmitter (table B1). Once transmitters began to fail, the remaining transmitters died soon thereafter as was indicated by the survival distribution function (fig. B1).

Table B1. Descriptive statistics of transmitter life measured during tag life studies conducted at Little Goose Dam during the 2009 study periods. Transmitter model NTC-3-1 was used in yearling Chinook salmon and juvenile steelhead; model NTC-M-2 was used in subyearling Chinook salmon.

Transmitter type	Number of tags	Mean tag life	Standard deviation	Minimum tag life	Maximum tag life
NTC-3-1	48	18.6	1.6	13.4	22.2
NTC-M-2	49	21.3	3.4	4.8	24.3

The comparison of cumulative travel times from release to the detection arrays and the survival distribution function resulted in overall high probabilities of the transmitters being operational when the fish reached the arrays. During the spring, the lowest mean probability of the tags being functional for yearling Chinook salmon was 0.9987 for travel time from Little Goose Dam tailrace to downstream arrays; for juvenile steelhead the probability for Central Ferry to downstream arrays was lowest at 0.9973 (table B2). Subyearling Chinook salmon cumulative travel time was lowest for Central Ferry to downstream arrays at 0.9866 (table B2). The high probability of a tag being operational in all reaches suggests that the majority of fish would reach the arrays with a functional transmitter before a significant decline in the tags survival distribution function (fig. B1).

Table B2. Mean probability of transmitters being operational [$\hat{P}(L_{ij})$] when passing telemetry arrays used in the survival study conducted at Little Goose Dam during 2009.

Species	Reach	Mean	SD
Yearling Chinook salmon	Central Ferry to dam	1.0000	0.0007
	Central Ferry to downstream arrays	0.9990	0.0153
	Tailrace to downstream arrays	0.9987	0.0268
Juvenile steelhead	Central Ferry to dam	1.0000	0.0007
	Central Ferry to downstream arrays	0.9973	0.0462
	Tailrace to downstream arrays	0.9989	0.0221
Subyearling Chinook salmon	Central Ferry to dam	0.9973	0.0132
	Central Ferry to downstream arrays	0.9866	0.0218
	Tailrace to downstream arrays	0.9942	0.0170

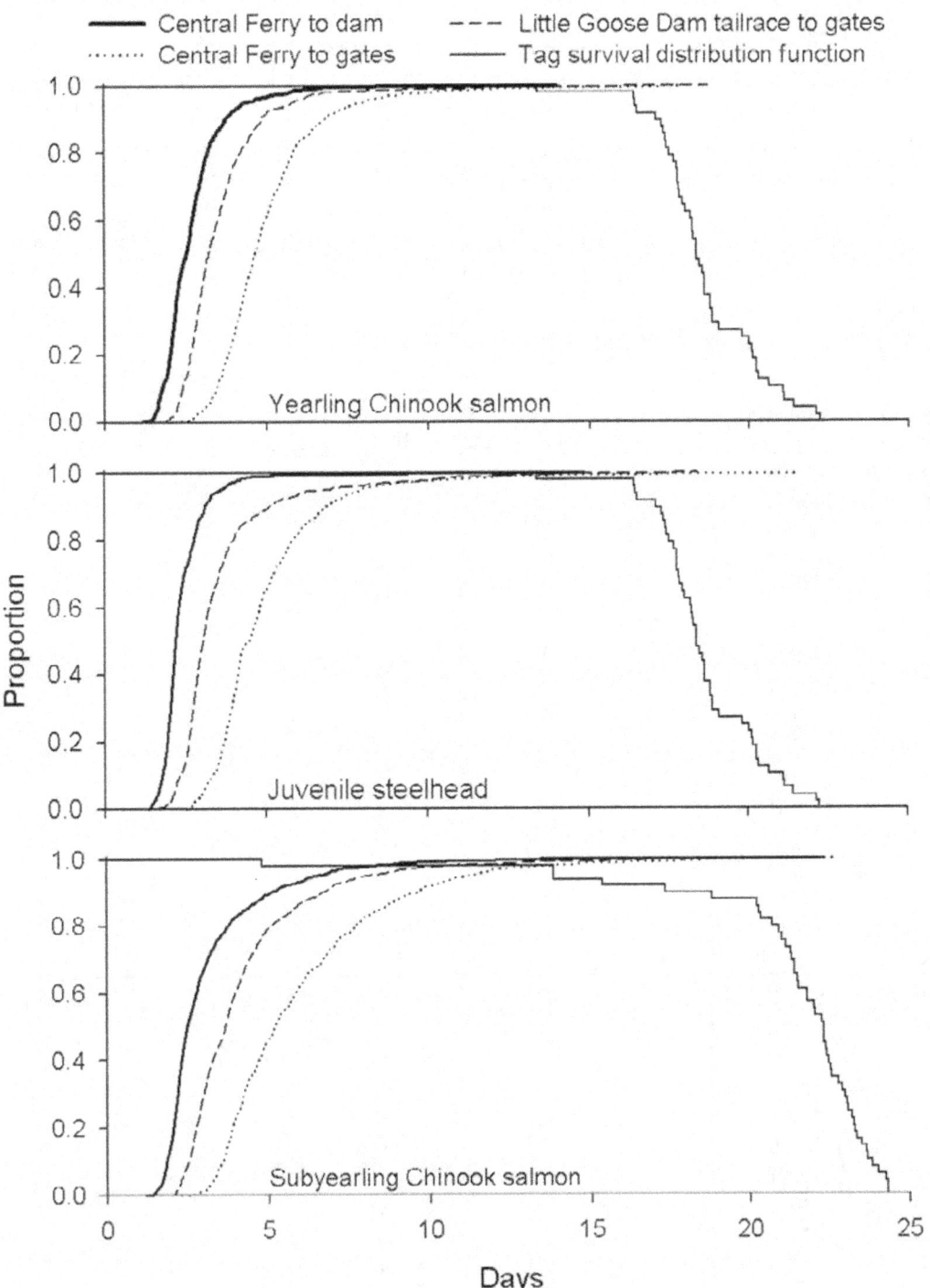

Figure B1. Graphs showing cumulative travel time distributions of radio-tagged fish compared to the survival distribution function for transmitter battery life at Little Goose Dam, 2009. Yearling Chinook salmon and juvenile steelhead cumulative travel times are compared to the survival distribution for model NTC-3-1 transmitters. Subyearling Chinook salmon cumulative travel times are compared to the survival distribution for model NTC-M-2 transmitters. Travel time distributions include the total elapsed time that the transmitter was operating prior to release of the fish.

Appendix C. Route-Specific Survival Estimates and Passage.

Table C1. Counts of detection histories of radio-tagged yearling Chinook salmon (CH1) and juvenile steelhead (HST) used in the route-specific survival models, Little Goose Dam, spring 2009. The detection history, composed of six digits, indicates (1) the release site (1 = Central Ferry, 0 = Little Goose Dam tailrace), (2) whether fish were detected (1) or not detected (0) at the forebay entrance array, (3) passage route for each fish (0 = unknown, 1 = released in tailrace, 2 = spillway, 3 = temporary spillway weir (TSW), 4 = bypass, 5 = turbine), and (4) whether fish were detected or not detected at each of three detection arrays downstream of Little Goose Dam. Counts of within-route double-array histories indicate the number of fish detected only on array 1 (10), only on array 2 (01), and on both array 1 and 2 (11). N = total number of fish detected passing via the indicated route.

Passage route	Detection history	Counts CH1 Day	Counts CH1 Night	Counts HST Day	Counts HST Night	History	Double CH1 Day	Double CH1 Night	Double HST Day	Double HST Night
Unknown	100000	13	6	7	5					
	110000	1	1	2	1					
	100100	0	0	0	0					
	110100	0	0	0	0					
	100010	0	0	0	0					
	110010	0	0	0	0					
	100001	0	0	0	0					
	110001	0	0	0	0					
	100110	0	0	0	0					
	110110	0	0	0	0					
	100101	0	0	0	0					
	110101	0	0	0	0					
	100011	0	0	0	0					
	110011	0	0	2	1					
	100111	0	0	0	0					
	110111	3	3	5	2					
N =		17	10	16	9					
Spillway	102000	0	0	0	0	10	9	0	2	3
	112000	5	2	0	1	01	0	0	0	0
	102100	0	0	0	0	11	50	25	16	58
	112100	0	0	0	0					
	102010	0	0	0	0					
	112010	1	0	0	0					
	102001	0	0	0	0					
	112001	0	1	0	0					
	102110	0	0	0	0					
	112110	1	0	1	1					
	102101	0	0	0	0					
	112101	2	0	2	3					
	102011	1	0	0	0					
	112011	5	0	1	1					
	102111	2	1	1	6					
	112111	42	21	13	49					
N =		59	25	18	61					

Passage route	Detection history	Counts				Within-route double array history counts				
		CH1		HST		History	CH1		HST	
		Day	Night	Day	Night		Day	Night	Day	Night
TSW	103000	0	0	0	0	10	1	1	1	0
	113000	16	2	1	1	01	1	0	1	0
	103100	0	0	0	0	11	370	152	326	85
	113100	2	0	1	0					
	103010	0	0	0	0					
	113010	0	1	1	0					
	103001	0	1	0	0					
	113001	0	1	0	0					
	103110	0	0	0	0					
	113110	7	4	6	2					
	103101	0	0	0	0					
	113101	2	0	3	2					
	103011	2	2	1	0					
	113011	8	4	23	2					
	103111	14	7	11	2					
	113111	321	131	281	76					
$N =$		372	153	328	85					
Bypass	104000	0	0	0	0	10	0	1	1	1
	114000	1	3	2	1	01	1	0	1	0
	104100	0	0	0	0	11	104	91	125	215
	114100	0	2	0	1					
	104010	0	0	0	2					
	114010	1	0	0	0					
	104001	0	0	1	0					
	114001	1	0	0	0					
	104110	3	0	0	0					
	114110	0	0	0	2					
	104101	0	0	3	0					
	114101	1	0	4	4					
	104011	0	0	2	1					
	114011	2	3	8	4					
	104111	3	2	7	14					
	114111	93	82	100	187					
$N =$		105	92	127	216					

Table C1 continued.

| Passage route | Detection history | Counts | | | | Within-route double array history counts | | | | |
| | | CH1 | | HST | | | CH1 | | HST | |
		Day	Night	Day	Night	History	Day	Night	Day	Night
Turbine	105000	0	0	0	0	10	0	1	0	0
	115000	1	3	0	0	01	0	0	0	0
	105100	0	0	0	0	11	13	19	2	9
	115100	1	0	0	0					
	105010	0	0	0	0					
	115010	0	0	0	0					
	105001	0	0	0	0					
	115001	0	0	0	0					
	105110	0	0	0	0					
	115110	0	0	0	0					
	105101	0	0	0	0					
	115101	0	1	0	1					
	105011	0	0	0	0					
	115011	0	1	0	0					
	105111	2	1	0	0					
	115111	9	14	2	8					
$N =$		13	20	2	9					
Control	001111	268	256	247	269					
	001110	3	4	4	4					
	001101	2	1	11	7					
	001100	1	3	1	1					
	001011	11	15	27	6					
	001010	0	0	0	0					
	001001	0	1	3	1					
	001000	8	13	0	3					
$N =$		293	293	293	291					

88

Table C2. Counts of detection histories of radio-tagged subyearling Chinook salmon used in the route-specific survival model, Little Goose Dam, summer 2009. The detection history, composed of 5 digits, indicates (1) the release site (1 = Central Ferry, 0 = Little Goose Dam tailrace), (2) whether fish were detected (1) or not detected (0) at the forebay entrance array, (3) the route of passage for each fish (0 = not detected, 1 = released in tailrace, 2 = spillway, 3 = temporary spillway weir (TSW), 4 = bypass, 5 = turbine), and (4) whether fish were detected or not detected at two detection arrays downstream of Little Goose Dam. Counts of within-route double-array histories indicate the number of fish detected only on array 1 (10), only on array 2 (01), and on both array 1 and 2 (11). N = total number of fish detected passing via the indicated route.

Passage route	Detection history	Counts		Within-route double array history counts		
		Day	Night	History	Day	Night
Unknown	10000	137	61			
	10010	1	0			
	10001	4	2			
	10011	1	6			
	11000	27	8			
	11010	2	0			
	11001	0	1			
	11011	10	13			
$N =$		182	91			
Spillway	10200	5	3	10	12	12
	10210	0	0	01	0	0
	10201	2	1	11	68	57
	10211	9	1			
	11200	16	14			
	11210	6	5			
	11201	5	2			
	11211	37	43			
$N =$		80	69			
TSW	10300	41	14	10	23	3
	10310	20	4	01	12	7
	10301	22	3	11	1,118	235
	10311	142	30			
	11300	124	26			
	11310	80	16			
	11301	72	14			
	11311	652	138			
$N =$		1,153	245			

Table C2 continued.

Passage route	Detection history	Counts		Within-route double array history counts		
		Day	Night	History	Day	Night
Bypass	10400	12	11	10	0	2
	10410	3	7	01	4	2
	10401	2	4	11	232	288
	10411	23	25			
	11400	42	37			
	11410	18	18			
	11401	10	8			
	11411	126	182			
$N =$		236	292			
Turbine	10500	0	6	10	3	9
	10510	1	1	01	0	0
	10501	0	0	11	11	71
	10511	3	11			
	11500	4	15			
	11510	2	6			
	11501	0	2			
	11511	4	39			
$N =$		14	80			
Control	00100	97	119			
	00110	73	74			
	00101	76	66			
	00111	558	569			
$N =$		804	828			

Table C3. Model summary of single-release model comparisons for yearling Chinook salmon (CH1), juvenile steelhead (HST), and subyearling Chinook salmon (CH0) in which survival estimates for the pool, forebay, dam, or control reaches were assumed to be equal or not equal among four taggers, Little Goose Dam, 2009. Asterisks indicate cases where the most parsimonious model assumed a difference in radio-tagged fish survival among tag taggers. AIC = Akaike's Information Criterion.

Species	Model	Number of parameters	AIC	Delta AIC	Model likelihood	Model weight
CH1	S pool equal	29	307.9	0.00	1.00	0.83
	S pool not equal	32	311.0	3.12	0.21	0.17
	S fb equal	32	316.0	4.94	0.08	0.08
	S fb not equal	32	311.0	0.00	1.00	0.92*
	S concrete equal	29	309.5	0.00	1.00	0.68
	S concrete not equal	32	311.0	1.50	0.47	0.32
	$S1$con equal	29	311.5	0.43	0.80	0.45
	$S1$con not equal	32	311.0	0.00	1.00	0.55
HST	S pool equal	22	291.7	0.00	1.00	0.87
	S pool not equal	25	295.5	3.75	0.15	0.13
	S fb equal	24	298.3	2.84	0.24	0.19
	S fb not equal	25	295.5	0.00	1.00	0.81*
	S concrete equal	22	290.8	0.00	1.00	0.91
	S concrete not equal	25	295.5	4.70	0.10	0.09
	$S1$con equal	25	302.9	7.48	0.02	0.02
	$S1$con not equal	25	295.5	0.00	1.00	0.98*
CH0	S pool equal	27	423.7	0.00	1.00	0.92
	S pool not equal	30	428.5	4.80	0.09	0.08
	S fb equal	27	422.8	0.00	1.00	0.95
	S fb not equal	30	428.5	5.77	0.06	0.05
	S concrete equal	27	431.0	2.50	0.29	0.22
	S concrete not equal	30	428.5	0.00	1.00	0.78*
	$S1$con equal	27	423.3	0.00	1.00	0.93
	$S1$con not equal	30	428.5	5.19	0.07	0.07

Table C4. Single-release survival estimates for reaches from the point of passage at Little Goose Dam or the control release site in the tailrace to the first downstream detection array, 2009. Reach lengths from the dam to the first downstream detection array were 29 km for yearling Chinook salmon and juvenile hatchery steelhead, and 40 km for subyearling Chinook salmon. Estimates, standard errors (SE) and 95% profile likelihood confidence intervals (95% PCI) are presented.

Species	Passage route	Day		Night		Overall	
		Estimate(SE)	95% PCI	Estimate(SE)	95% PCI	Estimate(SE)	95% PCI
Yearling Chinook	TSW	0.957(0.011)	0.933,0.975	0.987(0.009)	0.961,0.998	0.967(0.008)	0.950,0.980
	Spillway	0.915(0.036)	0.827,0.969	0.920(0.054)	0.773,0.982	0.917(0.030)	0.845,0.963
	Bypass	0.990(0.009)	0.959,0.999	0.969(0.019)	0.919,0.993	0.983(0.009)	0.959,0.995
	Turbine	0.923(0.074)	0.703,0.995	0.850(0.080)	0.656,0.958	0.898(0.056)	0.744,0.970
	Control	0.973(0.010)	0.950,0.988	0.956(0.012)	0.928,0.976	0.967(0.007)	0.950,0.980
Juvenile Steelhead	TSW	0.997(0.003)	0.987,1.000	0.988(0.012)	0.949,0.999	0.993(0.005)	0.976,0.999
	Spillway	1.000(0.000)	1.000,1.000	0.984(0.016)	0.930,0.999	0.993(0.007)	0.969,1.000
	Bypass	0.984(0.011)	0.952,0.998	0.995(0.005)	0.980,1.000	0.989(0.007)	0.971,0.997
	Turbine	1.000(0.000)	1.000,1.000	1.000(0.000)	1.000,1.000	1.000(0.000)	1.000,1.000
	Control	1.000(0.000)	1.000,1.000	0.990(0.006)	0.974,0.998	0.996(0.003)	0.988,0.999
Subyearling Chinook	TSW	0.868(0.011)	0.847,0.888	0.845(0.024)	0.795,0.888	0.861(0.010)	0.839,0.880
	Spillway	0.747(0.050)	0.643,0.836	0.761(0.052)	0.650,0.853	0.752(0.038)	0.673,0.820
	Bypass	0.781(0.028)	0.724,0.832	0.844(0.022)	0.798,0.884	0.801(0.020)	0.760,0.839
	Turbine	0.724(0.122)	0.461,0.913	0.745(0.050)	0.641,0.834	0.730(0.085)	0.549,0.864
	Control	0.891(0.012)	0.867,0.912	0.865(0.012)	0.840,0.888	0.882(0.009)	0.865,0.898

Appendix D. Dam Operations and River Conditions

Table D1. Spill pattern tables used with the low elevation spillway weir crest, Little Goose Dam, 2009 (data from Sean Milligan, U.S. Army Corps of Engineers, Walla Walla District). The spill pattern was run-of-river through the TSW and uniform training spill through spill bays 2–8.

Table LGS-10. Little Goose Dam spill pattern for low crest (Crest Elev. = 618 ft) Spillway Weir.

PH (kcfs)	Spill (kcfs)	Calc River (kcfs)	Percent Spill	Forebay WSE (ft) (Note 2)	Powerhouse Flow (kcfs) [Notes 1 and 2]						Spillway Flow (steps) [Note 2]								Total Steps, TS	Notes
					1 (Nt 2)	2	3	4	5	6	1	2	3	4	5	6	7	8		
27.3	11.3	39.6	31.1%	634.5	160	113					SW-LO								0	Lowest Qt possible w/ SW-LO (Note 5)
31.7	12.3	44.0	28.0%	634.5	160	157					SW-LO								0	
30.0	14.1	44.1	31.9%	634.5	160	140					SW-LO	1							1	Max. Qt for MOP=1 rules to apply (Note 2)
34.9	14.1	49.0	28.7%	634.5	175	174					SW-LO	1							1	Max Qt for MOP rules to apply (Note 2)
34.3	14.7	49.0	30.0%	633.5	172	171	113				SW-LO	1	1						2	
38.6	16.5	55.1	29.0%	633.5	160	113	113				SW-LO	1	1	1					3	
42.5	18.2	60.7	30.0%	633.5	160	133	132				SW-LO	1	1	1	1				4	
46.6	20.0	66.6	30.0%	633.5	160	153	153				SW-LO	1	1	1	1	1			5	
50.6	21.7	72.3	30.0%	633.5	169	169	168				SW-LO	1	1	1	1	1	1		6	Likely lowest Qt w/ SW-LO (Note 6)
54.7	23.5	78.2	30.0%	633.5	160	124	124	113.9			SW-LO	1	1	1	1	1	1	1	7	
59.1	25.3	84.4	30.0%	633.5	160	144	144	143			SW-LO	2	1	1	1	1	1	1	8	
63.5	27.2	90.7	30.0%	633.5	160	159	158	158			SW-LO	2	2	1	1	1	1	1	9	
67.0	29.1	97.0	30.0%	633.5	170	170	170	169			SW-LO	2	2	2	1	1	1	1	10	
72.4	31.0	103.4	30.0%	633.5	160	141	141	141	141		SW-LO	2	2	2	2	1	1	1	11	
76.8	32.9	109.7	30.0%	633.5	160	152	152	152	152		SW-LO	2	2	2	2	2	1	1	12	
81.2	34.8	116.0	30.0%	633.5	163	163	162	162	162		SW-LO	2	2	2	2	2	2	1	13	
85.6	36.7	122.3	30.0%	633.5	172	171	171	171	171		SW-LO	2	2	2	2	2	2	2	14	
90.2	38.7	128.9	30.0%	633.5	160	149	149	148	148	148	SW-LO	2	2	2	2	2	2	2	15	
94.9	40.7	135.6	30.0%	633.5	160	158	158	158	158	157	SW-LO	3	2	2	2	2	2	2	16	
99.5	42.7	142.2	30.0%	633.5	166	166	166	166	166	165	SW-LO	3	3	2	2	2	2	2	17	
104.2	44.6	148.8	30.0%	633.5	174	174	174	174	173	173	SW-LO	3	3	3	2	2	2	2	18	
108.8	46.6	155.4	30.0%	633.5	175	175	175	188	188	187	SW-LO	3	3	3	3	3	2	2	19	Max. PH capacity w/ Qt=30%, (Note 7)
109.2	48.6	157.8	30.8%	633.5	175	175	175	189	189	189	SW-LO	3	3	3	3	3	3	3	20	
109.2	50.6	159.8	31.7%	633.5	175	175	175	189	189	189	SW-LO	3	3	3	3	3	3	3	21	
109.2	52.6	161.8	32.5%	633.5	175	175	175	189	189	189	SW-LO	4	3	3	3	3	3	3	22	
109.2	54.5	163.7	33.3%	633.5	175	175	175	189	189	189	SW-LO	4	4	3	3	3	3	3	23	
109.2	56.5	165.7	34.1%	633.5	175	175	175	189	189	189	SW-LO	4	4	4	3	3	3	3	24	

93

Table D1 continued.

PH (kcfs)	Spill (kcfs)	Cnk River (kcfs)	Per-cent Spill	Forebay WSE (ft) (Note 2)	Powerhouse Flow (kcfs) [Notes 1 and 2]						Spillway Flow (stops) [Note 2]								Total Stops TS	Notes
					1 (Nt 3)	2	3	4	5	6	1	2	3	4	5	6	7	8		
109.2	58.5	167.7	34.9%	633.5	17.5	17.5	17.5	18.9	18.9	18.9	SW-LO	4	4	4	4	3	3	3	25	
109.2	60.4	169.6	35.6%	633.5	17.5	17.5	17.5	18.9	18.9	18.9	SW-LO	4	4	4	4	4	3	3	26	
109.2	62.4	171.6	36.4%	633.5	17.5	17.5	17.5	18.9	18.9	18.9	SW-LO	4	4	4	4	4	4	3	27	
109.2	64.3	173.5	37.1%	633.5	17.5	17.5	17.5	18.9	18.9	18.9	SW-LO	4	4	4	4	4	4	4	28	
109.2	66.3	175.5	37.8%	633.5	17.5	17.5	17.5	18.9	18.9	18.9	SW-LO	5	4	4	4	4	4	4	29	
109.2	68.2	177.4	38.5%	633.5	17.5	17.5	17.5	18.9	18.9	18.9	SW-LO	5	5	4	4	4	4	4	30	
109.2	70.2	179.4	39.1%	633.5	17.5	17.5	17.5	18.9	18.9	18.9	SW-LO	5	5	5	4	4	4	4	31	
109.2	72.1	181.3	39.8%	633.5	17.5	17.5	17.5	18.9	18.9	18.9	SW-LO	5	5	5	5	4	4	4	32	
109.2	74.1	183.3	40.4%	633.5	17.5	17.5	17.5	18.9	18.9	18.9	SW-LO	5	5	5	5	5	4	4	33	
109.2	76.0	185.2	41.0%	633.5	17.5	17.5	17.5	18.9	18.9	18.9	SW-LO	5	5	5	5	5	5	4	34	
109.2	78.0	187.2	41.7%	633.5	17.5	17.5	17.5	18.9	18.9	18.9	SW-LO	5	5	5	5	5	5	5	35	
109.2	79.9	189.1	42.3%	633.5	17.5	17.5	17.5	18.9	18.9	18.9	SW-LO	6	5	5	5	5	5	5	36	
109.2	81.9	191.1	42.9%	633.5	17.5	17.5	17.5	18.9	18.9	18.9	SW-LO	6	6	5	5	5	5	5	37	
109.2	83.8	193.0	43.4%	633.5	17.5	17.5	17.5	18.9	18.9	18.9	SW-LO	6	6	6	5	5	5	5	38	
109.2	85.8	195.0	44.0%	633.5	17.5	17.5	17.5	18.9	18.9	18.9	SW-LO	6	6	6	6	5	5	5	39	
109.2	87.7	196.9	44.5%	633.5	17.5	17.5	17.5	18.9	18.9	18.9	SW-LO	6	6	6	6	6	5	5	40	
109.2	89.7	198.9	45.1%	633.5	17.5	17.5	17.5	18.9	18.9	18.9	SW-LO	6	6	6	6	6	6	5	41	
109.2	91.6	200.8	45.6%	633.5	17.5	17.5	17.5	18.9	18.9	18.9	SW-LO	6	6	6	6	6	6	6	42	
109.2	93.6	202.8	46.1%	633.5	17.5	17.5	17.5	18.9	18.9	18.9	SW-LO	7	6	6	6	6	6	6	43	
109.2	95.5	204.7	46.7%	633.5	17.5	17.5	17.5	18.9	18.9	18.9	SW-LO	7	7	6	6	6	6	6	44	
109.2	97.5	206.7	47.2%	633.5	17.5	17.5	17.5	18.9	18.9	18.9	SW-LO	7	7	7	6	6	6	6	45	
109.2	99.4	208.6	47.6%	633.5	17.5	17.5	17.5	18.9	18.9	18.9	SW-LO	7	7	7	7	6	6	6	46	
109.2	101.3	210.5	48.1%	633.5	17.5	17.5	17.5	18.9	18.9	18.9	SW-LO	7	7	7	7	7	6	6	47	
109.2	103.3	212.5	48.6%	633.5	17.5	17.5	17.5	18.9	18.9	18.9	SW-LO	7	7	7	7	7	7	6	48	
109.2	105.2	214.4	49.1%	633.5	17.5	17.5	17.5	18.9	18.9	18.9	SW-LO	7	7	7	7	7	7	7	49	
109.2	107.2	216.4	49.5%	633.5	17.5	17.5	17.5	18.9	18.9	18.9	SW-LO	8	7	7	7	7	7	7	50	
109.2	109.1	218.3	50.0%	633.5	17.5	17.5	17.5	18.9	18.9	18.9	SW-LO	8	8	7	7	7	7	7	51	
109.2	111.1	220.3	50.4%	633.5	17.5	17.5	17.5	18.9	18.9	18.9	SW-LO	8	8	8	7	7	7	7	52	
109.2	113.0	222.2	50.9%	633.5	17.5	17.5	17.5	18.9	18.9	18.9	SW-LO	8	8	8	8	7	7	7	53	

Table D2. Summary statistics for discharge through the total project, powerhouse, spillway, and TSW and percent spill at Little Goose Dam during spring and summer 2009.

Season	Dam area	Mean	Median	Min	Max	SD
Spring	Total Project	111.56	103.51	60.94	164.88	29.16
	Powerhouse	79.69	72.19	42.85	111.49	22.35
	TSW	11.10	11.08	10.52	11.99	0.19
	Spillway (bays 2–8)	20.77	18.49	7.37	44.19	8.20
	Percent spill (bays 1–8)	28.88	30.10	17.64	35.34	3.18
Summer	Total Project	93.65	91.59	43.69	164.85	25.49
	Powerhouse	65.93	63.80	28.99	109.79	18.86
	TSW	11.15	11.14	10.65	11.63	0.19
	Spillway (bays 2–8)	16.57	16.63	3.69	46.01	7.33
	Percent spill (bays 1–8)	29.79	30.37	21.20	35.78	2.12

Table D3. Summary statistics for forebay elevation (NGVD 29), total dissolved gas, and water temperature at Little Goose Dam, 2009 and the 10-year average, during spring and summer study periods.

Season	Measurement	Year	Mean	Median	Min.	Max.	SD
Spring	Elevation (ft)	2009	633.41	633.40	632.87	634.23	0.18
		1999–2008	633.75	633.74	633.64	633.88	0.06
	Total dissolved gas (%)	2009	110.82	108.73	104.06	126.09	5.57
		1999–2008	108.93	107.96	106.15	113.81	2.08
	Temperature (°C)	2009	10.67	10.78	8.07	13.02	1.53
		1999–2008	11.37	11.23	9.44	13.47	1.11
Summer	Elevation (ft)	2009	633.46	633.45	633.00	633.90	0.17
		1999–2008	633.83	633.84	633.72	633.96	0.06
	Total dissolved gas (%)	2009	109.36	109.12	105.02	115.73	2.94
		1999–2008	109.02	109.14	106.48	111.74	1.30
	Temperature (°C)	2009	15.54	15.51	13.20	19.32	1.67
		1999–2008	15.61	15.45	13.39	18.88	1.65

Appendix E. Forebay Residence Time

Table E1. Forebay residence time of radio-tagged yearling Chinook salmon, juvenile steelhead, and subyearling Chinook salmon by diel period at Little Goose Dam, 2009. Fish with unknown passage routes were censored at time of last forebay detection. Forebay residence time is for the 2 km forebay until passage. Fish with unknown passage were censored.

Species	Diel period	N	Mean ± SE	Median (95% CI)	Min.	90th	Max.
Yearling Chinook salmon	Day	521	10.44 ± 0.63	6.73 (6.19– 7.32)	0.25	21.17	174.40
	Night	291	9.19 ± 0.90	5.03 (4.48– 5.53)	1.05	17.80	178.54
Juvenile steelhead	Day	636	12.55 ± 0.59	8.43 (7.79– 9.03)	0.08	25.36	151.05
	Night	177	10.50 ± 0.91	5.61 (4.54– 6.41)	1.19	24.28	68.45
Subyearling Chinook salmon	Day	1,406	12.38 ± 0.51	5.36 (5.03– 5.79)	0.02	26.67	256.98
	Night	454	18.92 ± 1.61	6.32 (5.09– 7.47)	0.30	48.88	282.72

Table E2. Forebay residence time of radio-tagged yearling Chinook salmon, juvenile steelhead, and subyearling Chinook salmon overall and by known passage routes at Little Goose Dam, 2009. One yearling Chinook salmon passed via the adult ladder. Forebay residence time is for the 2 km forebay until passage. Fish with unknown passage were censored in the overall estimates.

Species	Passage route	N	Mean ± SE	Median (95% CI)	Min.	90th	Max.
Yearling Chinook salmon	Spillway	80	7.61 ± 1.74	3.95 (3.29– 4.49)	1.23	13.95	136.40
	TSW	499	8.92 ± 0.52	5.53 (5.04– 6.12)	1.05	18.10	178.54
	Bypass	195	12.76 ± 1.36	7.72 (6.81– 9.49)	1.98	21.82	174.39
	Turbine	30	12.04 ± 2.03	7.55 (5.71– 11.68)	1.76	24.84	42.93
	Overall	812	10.00 ± 0.52	6.02 (5.58– 6.55)	0.25	19.81	178.54
Juvenile steelhead	Spillway	72	10.78 ± 1.22	8.65 (5.64– 11.20)	1.83	17.31	65.17
	TSW	399	10.02 ± 0.65	5.87 (5.35– 6.32)	1.11	20.11	125.72
	Bypass	318	14.3 ± 0.84	10.05 (9.10– 10.83)	1.87	29.02	151.05
	Turbine	11	14.84 ± 4.85	8.61 (3.92– 18.16)	2.82	18.16	47.65
	Overall	813	12.11 ± 0.50	7.80 (7.35– 8.36)	0.08	25.12	151.05
Subyearling Chinook salmon	Spillway	128	13.60 ± 2.06	5.31 (3.92– 6.16)	0.99	27.21	131.51
	TSW	1,122	11.30 ± 0.67	4.00 (3.78– 4.37)	0.78	22.07	216.76
	Bypass	477	17.77 ± 1.29	9.41 (8.73– 10.84)	1.63	38.26	282.72
	Turbine	72	11.20 ± 1.32	6.78 (5.40– 9.89)	1.62	21.51	70.50
	Overall	1,860	13.98 ± 0.61	5.43 (5.18– 5.87)	0.02	31.17	282.72

Appendix F. Synopsis.

<u>Year</u>: 2009

<u>Study site</u>: Little Goose Dam

<u>Objectives of study</u>:
1. Determine the approach path, route of passage, and tailrace egress of spring and summer migrants relative to post-construction of the temporary spillway weir (TSW)
2. Estimate route-specific survival of spring and summer migrants through Little Goose Dam

<u>Fish</u>:

Table F1. Summary statistics of fork length and weight of radio-tagged fish released at Little Goose Dam, 2009.

Species	Release group	N	Fork Length (mm)			Weight (g)		
			Mean	SD	Range	Mean	SD	Range
Yearling Chinook salmon	Treatment	883	139.3	11.2	115 – 195	26.7	7.2	14.4 – 70.3
	Control	587	139.1	11.5	110 – 226	26.6	7.0	14.3 – 53.4
	Euthanized	50	136.7	10.7	110 – 156	25.4	6.3	14.4 – 39.3
Juvenile steelhead	Treatment	880	214.2	23.5	113 – 275	90.3	29.2	19.7 – 205.6
	Control	587	215.1	21.7	112 – 284	90.1	28.5	14.2 – 216.4
	Euthanized	50	219.9	22.0	172 – 271	96.8	30.0	44.9 – 173.6
Subyearling Chinook salmon	Treatment	2,569	107.1	5.5	96 – 142	12.4	2.3	10.0 – 32.3
	Control	1,632	107.0	5.7	97 – 142	12.3	2.4	10.0 – 34.5
	Euthanized	50	107.7	6.6	100 – 132	12.6	2.9	10.1 – 25.6

All fish were collected by the Oregon Department of Fish and Wildlife during the daily sample for the Fish Passage Center.

<u>Transmitter</u>:
Spring- Lotek Wireless © radio transmitter model NTC-3-1 (0.64 g in air) with 16 cm "S1" antenna and 2.0 s burst rate and Biomark PIT tag model TX1411ST (0.10 g in air)
Summer- Lotek Wireless © radio transmitter model NTC-M-2 (0.43 g in air) with 16 cm "S1" antenna and 2.5 s burst rate and Biomark PIT tag model TX1411ST(0.10 g in air)

<u>Implant procedure</u>: All transmitters were surgically implanted

<u>Survival estimate</u>: Using Route-Specific Survival Model

Table F2. Overall passage and survival estimates of yearling Chinook salmon and juvenile steelhead at Little Goose Dam, spring 2009. Probabilities, standard errors (SE) and 95% profile likelihood confidence intervals (95% PCI) are presented.

	Parameters	Yearling Chinook salmon		Juvenile steelhead	
		Probability (SE)	95% PCI	Probability (SE)	95% PCI
Passage Probabilities	Spill bays 2–8	0.099(0.010)	0.080,0.121	0.092(0.010)	0.074,0.113
	TSW	0.625(0.017)	0.592,0.657	0.489(0.017)	0.455,0.522
	Bays 2–8 and TSW	0.724(0.015)	0.694,0.754	0.581(0.017)	0.548,0.614
	Bypass	0.237(0.015)	0.209,0.266	0.406(0.017)	0.374,0.439
	Turbine	0.039(0.007)	0.027,0.054	0.013(0.004)	0.007,0.022
	Powerhouse	0.276(0.015)	0.246,0.306	0.419(0.017)	0.386,0.452
	FGE	0.858(0.022)	0.809,0.899	0.969(0.009)	0.948,0.976
	FPE	0.961(0.007)	0.946,0.970	0.987(0.004)	0.978,0.989
Effectiveness	SPS bays 2–8 (*SPS*)	0.532(0.055)	0.431,0.647	0.495(0.053)	0.398,0.606
	TSW (*SOS*)	6.449(0.172)	6.370,6.600	5.060(0.177)	4.720,5.365
	All spill (*SPS*)	2.554(0.054)	2.445,2.658	2.049(0.060)	1.932,2.165
Survival Probabilities	Pool	0.978(0.005)	0.967,0.986	0.986(0.004)	0.977,0.993
	Forebay	0.998(0.002)	0.993,1.000	0.990(0.002)	0.990,0.999
	Spill bays 2–8	0.948(0.032)	0.873,1.000	0.997(0.008)	0.973,1.008
	TSW	1.001(0.011)	0.979,1.023	0.998(0.006)	0.980,1.008
	Bays 2–8 and TSW	0.993(0.011)	0.973,1.016	0.997(0.005)	0.984,1.007
	Bypass	1.016(0.012)	0.988,1.040	0.994(0.007)	0.975,1.005
	Turbine	0.928(0.058)	0.770,1.005	1.005(0.003)	1.001,1.012
	Powerhouse	1.004(0.014)	0.973,1.030	0.994(0.007)	0.975,1.005
	Dam	0.992(0.010)	0.971,1.013	0.994(0.004)	0.984,1.003
	Concrete	0.994(0.010)	0.974,1.015	0.998(0.004)	0.989,1.006

Table F3. Overall passage and survival estimates of subyearling Chinook salmon at Little Goose Dam, summer 2009. Probabilities, standard errors (SE) and 95% profile likelihood confidence intervals (95% PCI) are presented.

	Parameters	Subyearling Chinook salmon	
		Probability (SE)	95% PCI
Passage Probabilities	Spill bays 2–8	0.068(0.005)	0.058,0.079
	TSW	0.646(0.010)	0.627,0.666
	Bays 2–8 and TSW	0.714(0.010)	0.695,0.733
	Bypass	0.244(0.009)	0.226,0.262
	Turbine	0.042(0.004)	0.034,0.051
	Powerhouse	0.286(0.010)	0.267,0.305
	FGE	0.852(0.014)	0.824,0.879
	FPE	0.958(0.004)	0.949,0.960
Effectiveness	SPS bays 2–8 (*SPS*)	0.383(0.030)	0.326,0.445
	TSW (*SOS*)	5.431(0.085)	5.263,5.588
	All spill (*SPS*)	2.417(0.032)	2.352,2.480
Survival Probabilities	Pool	0.922(0.006)	0.911,0.933
	Forebay	0.984(0.003)	0.977,0.990
	Spill bays 2–8	0.852(0.044)	0.762,0.932
	TSW	0.975(0.015)	0.945,1.006
	Bays 2–8 and TSW	0.963(0.015)	0.934,0.991
	Bypass	0.908(0.024)	0.859,0.955
	Turbine	0.828(0.096)	0.623,0.980
	Powerhouse	0.898(0.024)	0.851,0.944
	Dam	0.936(0.013)	0.911,0.963
	Concrete	0.952(0.013)	0.926,0.978

Environmental/ operating conditions:

Table F4. Summary statistics for forebay elevation (NGVD 29), total dissolved gas and water temperature, at Little Goose Dam 2009 during spring and summer study periods.

Season	Measurement	Mean	Median	Min.	Max.	SD
Spring	Elevation (ft)	633.41	633.40	632.87	634.23	0.18
	Total dissolved gas (%)	110.82	108.73	104.06	126.09	5.57
	Temperature (°C)	10.67	10.78	8.07	13.02	1.53
Summer	Elevation (ft)	633.46	633.45	633.00	633.90	0.17
	Total dissolved gas (%)	109.36	109.12	105.02	115.73	2.94
	Temperature (°C)	15.54	15.51	13.20	19.32	1.67

Table F5. Summary statistics for discharge through the total project, powerhouse, spillway, and TSW and percent spill at Little Goose Dam during spring and summer 2009.

Season	Dam area	Mean	Median	Min	Max	SD
Spring	Total Project	111.56	103.51	60.94	164.88	29.16
	Powerhouse	79.69	72.19	42.85	111.49	22.35
	TSW	11.10	11.08	10.52	11.99	0.19
	Spillway (bays 2–8)	20.77	18.49	7.37	44.19	8.20
	Percent spill (bays 1–8)	28.88	30.10	17.64	35.34	3.18
Summer	Total Project	93.65	91.59	43.69	164.85	25.49
	Powerhouse	65.93	63.80	28.99	109.79	18.86
	TSW	11.15	11.14	10.65	11.63	0.19
	Spillway (bays 2–8)	16.57	16.63	3.69	46.01	7.33
	Percent spill (bays 1–8)	29.79	30.37	21.20	35.78	2.12

Unique study characteristics:

Structural modifications:

The trash/shear boom attachment was moved from the pier nose between spill bay 1 and spill bay 2 to the non-overflow section between the powerhouse and spillway.

A temporary spillway weir (TSW) was inserted into spill bay 1 at the low crest elevation of 188 m (618 ft; NGVD 29).

Operational:

Although the TSW was designed for operation at two weir elevations, the magnitude and timing of discharge didn't allow for changing the weir height to the high crest elevation, 190 m (622 ft; NGVD 29), until after all tagged fish were released.